focal POINT

NEW PAGE IDEAS AND
TECHNIQUES TO SHOWCASE
YOUR FAVORITE PHOTOS

THE EDITORS OF MEMORY MAKERS BOOKS

Memory Makers Books
Cincinnati, Ohio
www.memorymakersmagazine.com

10 09 08 07 06   5 4 3 2 1

Distributed in Canada by Fraser Direct
100 Armstrong Avenue
Georgetown, ON, Canada L7G 5S4
Tel: (905) 877-4411

Distributed in the U.K. and Europe by David & Charles
Brunel House, Newton Abbot, Devon, TQ12 4PU, England
Tel: (+44) 1626 323200, Fax: (+44) 1626 323319
E-mail: postmaster@davidandcharles.co.uk

Distributed in Australia by Capricorn Link
P.O. Box 704, S. Windsor, NSW 2756 Australia
Tel: (02) 4577-3555

Library of Congress Cataloging-in-Publication Data

Focal point : new page ideas and techniques to showcase
your favorite photos / From the Editors of Memory Makers
Books ; edited by Amy Glander. -- 1st ed.
       p. cm.
   Includes index.
   ISBN-13: 978-1-892127-96-9 (softcover : alk. paper)
   ISBN-10: 1-892127-96-2 (softcover : alk. paper)
   1. Photograph albums. 2. Scrapbooks. I. Glander, Amy,
1978- II. Memory Makers Books.
TR501.F63 2006
745.593--dc22
                                          2006026551

Editor: Amy Glander
Designer: Marissa Bowers
Layout Artist: Kathy Gardner
Production Coordinator: Matt Wagner
Photographers: Tim Grondin, Christine Polomsky

CONTRIBUTING ARTISTS

Joanna Bolick

Vicki Boutin

Nicole Cholet

Holly Corbett

Marie Cox

Kelly Goree

Greta Hammond

Linda Harrison

Sharon Laakkonen

Kelli Noto

Deb Perry

Suzy Plantamura

Torrey Scott

Shannon Taylor

Danielle Thompson

Courtney Walsh

CONTENTS

CHAPTER 3

EXTRAORDINARY EMBELLISHMENTS

56

CHAPTER 4

SENSATIONAL SURFACES

80

LET'S FACE IT. Without the photographs, scrapbooking would be nonexistent. Photographs teach us to view the world with a creative eye and allow us to tell our stories in a visual way. So much so, that as scrapbookers we've schooled ourselves in every element of photography from the principles of good composition to the intricate mechanical details of our camera. And as we get better, our snapshots begin to rival those seen on postcard racks in souvenir shops and the masterpieces gracing the pages of *National Geographic*. In short, we're getting pretty darn good.

But we're crafters, and that's simply not enough. We want to take our photos and turn them into something more than fodder for the albums stored in the front hall closet. It's time to look beyond the lens and see how your photos and scrapbook art can be approached in a whole new way. Within your hands is the essential source for taking the pictures you love and turning them into works of art through the use of innovative, hands-on altering techniques.

Focal Point offers a rich blend of information and inspiration for using your own artistic prowess to experiment with your favorite photos in new and exciting ways. You'll find fresh ways to crop, mat and frame photos; unique ideas for single photo pages and multiple photo pages; photo manipulation techniques such as distressing, tearing, inking, painting and digital effects; creative layouts for both black-and-white and color prints; unique ways to apply titles, journaling, borders and other design elements directly to photos; creative surfaces, photo transfer techniques and much, much more.

So turn the page and prepare to see stunning photography showcased in contemporary layouts that make the photo the star of the page!

being me

12.25.05

it only took 221 photos of you (roughly) to get this good shot!

despite this fact I do believe you are happier than you've ever been!

happiness

I love you so much it actuall

I think you are too darn cute! I am the m

I am proud of you everyday. Then th

A sweet DAY of HOPE joy laughter & LOVE Aaron & Shannon Feb 12 2006

tion-al (un'kən-dish'ən-'l), adj.

or reservations: absolute devotion

creative CROPPING

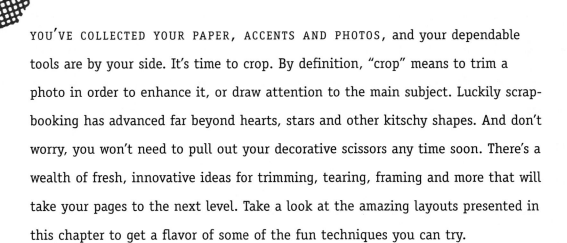

YOU'VE COLLECTED YOUR PAPER, ACCENTS AND PHOTOS, and your dependable tools are by your side. It's time to crop. By definition, "crop" means to trim a photo in order to enhance it, or draw attention to the main subject. Luckily scrapbooking has advanced far beyond hearts, stars and other kitschy shapes. And don't worry, you won't need to pull out your decorative scissors any time soon. There's a wealth of fresh, innovative ideas for trimming, tearing, framing and more that will take your pages to the next level. Take a look at the amazing layouts presented in this chapter to get a flavor of some of the fun techniques you can try.

Spring 2006

...on was an
...n learned
...You became
...ing saves)
...reat season!

WOW

dress

cute
♥fun

perfec

celebrate

DISCOVER

→	CROPPING	→	PHOTOMONTAGES
→	TEARING	→	FRAMING & MATTING
→	ABSTRACT PHOTO COLLAGE	→	PHOTO PUZZLES

CROPPING

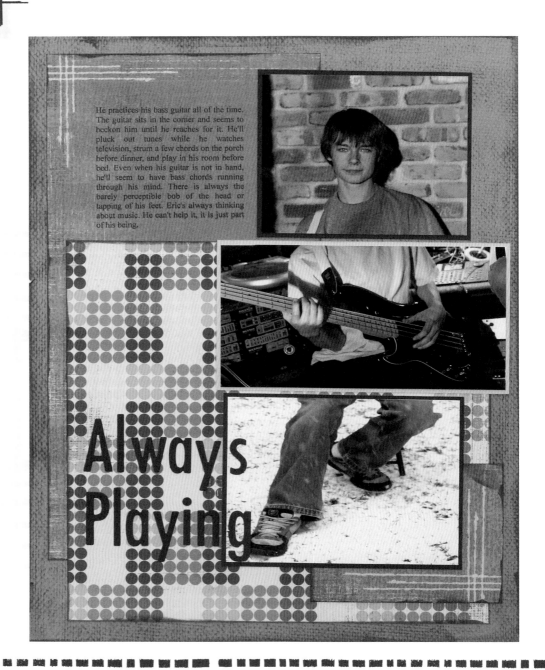

He practices his bass guitar all of the time. The guitar sits in the corner and seems to beckon him until he reaches for it. He'll pluck out tunes while he watches television, strum a few chords on the porch before dinner, and play in his room before bed. Even when his guitar is not in hand, he'll seem to have bass chords running through his mind. There is always the barely perceptible bob of the head or tapping of his feet. Eric's always thinking about music. He can't help it, it is just part of his being.

Always Playing

SUPPLIES: PATTERNED PAPER (ADORN IT); DIE-CUT LETTERS (QUICKUTZ); FLUID CHALK INK; CARDSTOCK

ALWAYS PLAYING

Kelli Noto,
Centennial, Colorado

Make a bold statement and play up the meaning of a page with this creative cropping technique. To emphasize her son's love for the guitar, Kelli cropped three different photos of him with his favorite instrument in hand. Using image-editing software, she strategically cropped the three photos with each serving as the top, middle and bottom to re-create his image. To save on photo paper, she lined the photos up in an 8" x 10" (20cm x 25cm) digital file and printed them. From head to toe, the photomontage shows that no matter the season, this boy is never without his guitar.

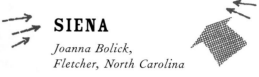

SUPPLIES: PATTERNED PAPER (AUTUMN LEAVES, SCENIC ROUTE PAPER CO., WE R MEMORY KEEPERS); RUBBER STAMPS (7 GYPSIES, MAKING MEMORIES); ACRYLIC STAMPS (AUTUMN LEAVES); CORNER ROUNDER; DYE INK; CARDSTOCK

SIENA

Joanna Bolick,
Fletcher, North Carolina

To zoom in on a photo subject or to remove distracting elements, try this creative cropping technique. Joanna simply turned over her photo and then lightly drew and numbered sections with a pencil. She cut out the marked pieces and then used a punch to round the corners of each section. Using the numbers as a guide, Joanna pieced the photo puzzle back together, including only the most relevant pieces.

HIGH SEAS LIVING

Shannon Taylor,
Bristol, Tennessee

The proof sheets that come with processed photos are good for more than taking photo inventory. The miniature size is perfect for making interesting photo mosaics and collages. Shannon cut individual photos from a proof sheet, retaining their white borders. She then strategically clustered and adhered the mini photos onto an old Central American map to highlight trip destinations. Use this technique to help tell your story by varying the way you cluster or collage the mini photos.

SUPPLIES: CHIPBOARD LETTERS (HEIDI SWAPP); CHIPBOARD ACCENTS (JUNKITZ); RUB-ON DOTS (CREATIVE IMAGINATIONS); MAP; BLACK PEN

TEARING

TAKE NOTE *For added definition and distressing, try inking the torn edges of the photo paper.*

SUPPLIES: PATTERNED PAPER, STICKER, RIBBONS, RUB-ONS, ACRYLIC "WAVE" ACCENT (KI MEMORIES); CARDSTOCK; TAHOMA FONT (MICROSOFT)

WAVES CRASHING

*Nicole Cholet,
Beaconsfield,
Quebec, Canada*

For a quick and easy way to crop a photo, just stitch and tear away. Nicole stitched her photo to the cardstock, making two rows of stitching for added stability. Then she tore the photo along the stitches, revealing the white core of the photo paper that mimics the crashing waves in the photos. The stitches guide the tearing and provide a barrier to prevent the cropping from going too far inward. This cropping-in-a-snap technique lends a timeless and worn feel.

EVERY
LITTLE
BIT

Even though I have had some hard times in my life … I am really thankful for them. Each experience, each little bit, has made me into the person that I am today. The good times, the the bad times … both are equally important in creating who I am . Even though I wish not to go through anymore dark times, I am thankful…

for every

single experience

SUPPLIES: PATTERNED
PAPER (SCRAPWORKS);
CORKBOARD FLOWERS (PRIMA);
LETTER STICKERS, COASTER
(IMAGINATION PROJECT); BRADS,
ACRYLIC FLOWER (QUEEN & CO.);
PEN; THREAD; CARDSTOCK

EVERY LITTLE BIT

Sharon Laakkonen,
Superior, Wisconsin

This unique tearing and piecing technique adds visual interest to a photo and offers an opportunity for self-reflection. Sharon created this innovative "photo-quilt" to represent both the good and bad times in life that together make her the whole person she is today. She printed her portrait twice: once in color and once in black-and-white. Placing the photos together, Sharon tore them at the same time. She then pieced the photo puzzle back together using a mix of black-and-white and colored pieces to represent both the happy and challenging times in her life.

SUPPLIES: PATTERNED PAPER (CRATE PAPER); BUTTONS (AUTUMN LEAVES); CHIPBOARD LETTERS (HEIDI SWAPP); ACRYLIC PAINT; THREAD; CARDSTOCK

NATURE

*Greta Hammond,
Goshen, Indiana*

When you'd like to highlight a photo subject, but the background is just as important in conveying the moment, try this clever tearing and piecing technique. Greta wanted to emphasize her daughter's image in the photo, but still keep the nature background. She tore the photo twice, cropping in as closely as possible. Next, she adhered the photo pieces to cardstock, leaving a slight gap to help emphasize her daughter. A triple-stitched border attaches the photo to the mat and adds a touch of texture.

SUPPLIES: PATTERNED PAPER (SCENIC ROUTE PAPER CO.); CHIPBOARD BRACKETS (HEIDI SWAPP); CHIPBOARD LETTERS (MAKING MEMORIES); CHIPBOARD FLOWER (IMAGINATION PROJECT); STAMPS (SCRAPTIVITY); PHOTO TURNS (7 GYPSIES); STAMPING INK; BROWN PEN; CARDSTOCK

LAYERS OF ME

Vicki Boutin,
Burlington, Ontario, Canada

A contemporary twist on a photo tearing technique creates a stunning focal photo. To achieve the funky layered effect, Vicki first printed three copies of her portrait in three different finishes: color, de-saturated and black-and-white. She tore the top half of the color photo and the bottom of the black-and-white photo, and then strategically placed the torn images over the full-size de-saturated photo for a seamless look. Try this technique to play up or play down a feature, such as Vicki did by using the torn color photo on top to bring out her baby-blues. The torn and layered technique echoes her title with a play on words, "Layers of Me."

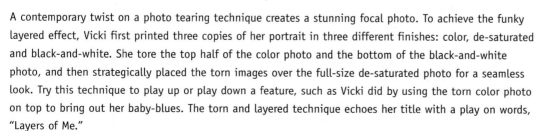

ABSTRACT PHOTO COLLAGE

SUPPLIES: PATTERNED PAPER (7 GYPSIES, SCENIC ROUTE PAPER CO.); GAFFER TAPE (7 GYPSIES); CHIPBOARD HEART, RUB-ON (IMAGINATION PROJECT); PHOTO CORNER (DAISY D'S); RICKRACK (JO-ANN STORES); PEN; BRAD; CLIPS; SEQUINS; DISTRESS INK

WARNING, I'M SEEING RED

Deb Perry,
Newport News, Virginia

An abstract photo collage enhanced with an eclectic mix of supplies plays up a page theme with punch and panache. Deb strategically layered blocks of patterned papers to serve as playful mats to her photo collage. After arranging her mix of small and large photos, she used tags, rickrack, rub-ons, sequins and paint all in shades of red to unify the piece. A red title boldly painted directly on the focal photo drives the spirited page theme with loads of whimsy.

TAKE NOTE *To add further interest, apply rub-ons and silhouettes directly on a photo.*

SUPPLIES: PATTERNED PAPER (CHERRY ARTE); CHIPBOARD LETTERS, SILHOUETTES, DECORATIVE TAPE, RUB-ONS, PUNCTUATION ACCENT (HEIDI SWAPP); EMBROIDERY FLOSS; PEN; CARDSTOCK

SPRING 06 SOCCER

Kelly Goree,
Shelbyville, Kentucky

This creative framing technique makes Kelly's photo collage burst with visual interest. Kelly resized her photos and changed a few to black-and-white before printing them. She rubbed the edges of the photos with a black ink pad for a defining grunge look. Using a template and cardstock, she created a star frame in which she arranged her photos. Some of the photos overlap the frame while others cleverly peek out from beneath.

PHOTOMONTAGE

TAKE NOTE *When creating photomontages, it's best to keep the design relatively simple so as not to overpower the layout.*

FACES

So many expressions…making faces all day long. Most times it's a big smile and for that I am so grateful, but other times I get the frown or the surprised look and even the pout. I love watching you make those silly faces.

SUPPLIES: PATTERNED PAPER, RUB-ONS (AMERICAN CRAFTS); CARDSTOCK

FACES

Marie Cox,
Raleigh, North Carolina

Creative cropping can add a punch of visual interest to a photomontage. Marie silhouette-cut portions of these three photos with a craft knife. Matted with patterned paper, the strategically placed silhouetted photos merge with the complementing background and rub-on title for a continuous photo series effect.

re:discovery

Going to the beach with you is like discovering it for the first time all over again.
Siesta Key Beach ~ 2005

SUPPLIES: PATTERNED PAPER (MY MIND'S EYE); BUTTONS (JO-ANN STORES); DIE-CUTS (QUICKUTZ); SHAKER SUN, BEADS (SOURCE UNKNOWN); PEN; CARDSTOCK

DISCOVERY

Linda Harrison,
Sarasota, Florida

Try this cutting and layering technique for a cool abstract photomontage. Linda printed three photos in varying sizes, and then trimmed her son's image from each photo in a variety of positions. She layered the three cutouts under and over wavy cut cardstock and patterned paper strips onto the background paper. The results are larger than life with the series of quirky cutouts adding action to the page.

FRAMING & MATTING

DADDY & NOAH

Holly Corbett,
Central, South Carolina

Though every photograph is precious, some deserve an extra special touch to make them stand out. For this photo of her husband nestling their newborn, Holly used a circle cutter to construct frames from black cardstock to create a mat resembling stained glass. The frames represent the leading between stained-glass panels, which are mimicked here with pastel vellum. She traced the inside of the frames onto the vellum to ensure a perfect fit. She placed the panels inside the frames, and then adhered them to the background, overlapping the circular designs. A stamped diamond pattern adds a touch of texture to the mat.

SUPPLIES: BACKGROUND STAMP (STAMPIN' UP); PHOTO CORNERS, BRADS (MAKING MEMORIES); RIBBON (MICHAELS); DIE-CUT LETTERS (QUICKUTZ); CIRCLE CUTTER; STAMPING INK; VELLUM; CARDSTOCK

PLAYING IN THE DIRT

Kelli Noto,
Centennial, Colorado

Distressed rub-ons work great for a quick grungy frame. Kelli cut a distressed border design from a sheet of rub-ons. She then placed the design onto the photo and rubbed it on with a wooden stick. Funky die-cut letters adhered directly over the photo serve as the title and also fill in an otherwise blank spot.

SUPPLIES: PATTERNED PAPER (ADORN IT); RUB-ON (KAREN RUSSELL); DIE-CUT LETTERS (QUICKUTZ); BRADS; CARDSTOCK

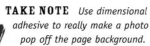

TAKE NOTE *Use dimensional adhesive to really make a photo pop off the page background.*

SUPPLIES: TEXTURED CARDSTOCK (PRISM); HOLE PUNCH; FOAM SPACERS; FELT PEN; FLUID CHALK INK; IMAGE EDITING SOFTWARE (ADOBE); MISTRAL TITLE FONT (MICROSOFT)

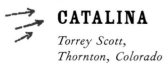

CATALINA

Torrey Scott,
Thornton, Colorado

Try this altering and layering technique for a fresh way to mat a photo with a true artistic touch. With image-editing software, Torrey duplicated her landscape photo, applied a charcoal filter and then printed the black-and-white image. She printed the original color version of the photo, and then silhouette-cut a portion of it. For definition, Torrey inked the edges of the silhouette and then mounted it strategically over the charcoal-like-sketch photo. The silhouetted image pops against the altered photo that doubles as an interesting mat.

SUPPLIES: PATTERNED PAPER (AUTUMN LEAVES, SANDYLION); RUB-ONS (ADORN IT, AUTUMN LEAVES, BASIC GREY); BUTTONS (AUTUMN LEAVES); RHINESTONES (DARICE, EK SUCCESS); SEQUINS; BEADS; BRADS (JUNKITZ, MAKING MEMORIES, SEI); RHINESTONE BRADS (MAKING MEMORIES); EMBROIDERY FLOSS; WHITE PEN

CELEBRATE

Suzy Plantamura,
Laguna Niguel, California

Add a spark of personality to a photo with this fresh framing technique. Suzy chose a photo with a plain background and cut the edges into wavy shapes. Contouring the wavy edges, she sewed buttons, sequins and beads, and adhered rhinestones and brads to frame the photo. She finished the photo treatment with a rub-on title applied directly on the photo. Serving dual purpose, this framing technique not only borders photos, it embellishes the page.

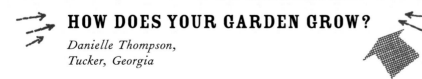

HOW DOES YOUR GARDEN GROW?

Danielle Thompson,
Tucker, Georgia

Make your photos pop with this whimsical framing treatment. Danielle used a circle cutter to create perfect circles from patterned papers. She handcut the flowers' petals and then adhered the frames over the photos with dimensional adhesive. The photos blossom with hand-stitched stems and hand-drawn leaves, and embellish the page with personality and texture.

SUPPLIES: PATTERNED PAPER (AUTUMN LEAVES, BO-BUNNY PRESS); LETTER STICKERS (AMERICAN CRAFTS, MAKING MEMORIES); PLASTIC LETTERS (HEIDI SWAPP); FILE TAB (AUTUMN LEAVES); EMBROIDERY FLOSS; MARKERS; FOAM TAPE; CIRCLE CUTTER; STAMPING INK

23

PHOTO PUZZLE

TAKE NOTE *For added fun, leave out a puzzle piece or adhere a piece out of place on the page.*

SUPPLIES: PATTERNED PAPER (AUTUMN LEAVES); LETTER STICKERS (SCRAPWORKS); RIBBON (AUTUMN LEAVES, MICHAELS); BUTTONS (FOOFALA); EMBROIDERY FLOSS; STAMPING INK; CARDSTOCK

PUTTING THE PIECES BACK TOGETHER

Courtney Walsh,
Winnebago, Illinois

Add a sense of fun or purpose to a photo subject with this playful puzzle technique. Courtney used this photo treatment to shed meaning on her page theme. She covered the back of her photo with adhesive and then matted it with chipboard timmed to the same size. With a cutting blade, she cut the photo into puzzle pieces. She adhered the pieces to the page one at a time, putting the puzzle together.

Repair Man   Father   BRAVE   My Rock

yOU PUZZLe me

SUPPLIES: PATTERNED PAPER, DECORATIVE HOOKS, RIBBON, FOAM STAMPS (JUNKITZ); CHIPBOARD LETTERS (HEIDI SWAPP); CANVAS ENVELOPE (MAKING MEMORIES); PAINT

YOU PUZZLE ME

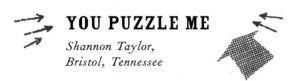

Shannon Taylor,
Bristol, Tennessee

This eye-pleasing technique is an easy and fun way to add to a photo story. Shannon placed a photo face down onto a light box and used a pen to draw puzzle shapes onto the back of the photo, beginning with a heart around her husband's face. Following her drawn puzzle pattern, she cut the photo into pieces with a scissors. She then adhered the puzzle to chipboard and cut out the matted pieces. She sanded the edges of each puzzle piece for definition before piecing it back together and adhering it to a cardstock mat.

artistic ALTERING

ALTERING A PHOTO WITH MATERIALS such as paint, ink or bleach may seem daunting at first. You may fear the results will not turn out as expected or you'll ruin precious photos. We urge you to put your fears to rest. With the birth of digital technology, you have the ability to scan or print multiple photos at your fingertips. The altering techniques in this chapter will open your eyes to a wealth of artistic possibilities. You'll discover new ways to enhance your photos with items in your scrapbook arsenal. You'll also find heritage layouts in this chapter to show that even treasured photos of yesteryear can be used with these creative techniques.

life is measured in

Moments

burs

You can **dance** ANYWHERE, even if only in your heart.

BeThany Ann

DISCOVER

PAINT	BOTTLED DYE INK
EMBOSSING INK	CHALK
INK PADS	BLEACH

SUPPLIES: PATTERNED PAPER, ACCENT RUB-ONS (BASIC GREY); RIBBON (MAYA ROAD); PAPER FLOWERS (PRIMA); BRADS (QUEEN & CO.); LETTER RUB-ONS (IMAGINATION PROJECT); ACRYLIC PAINT (DELTA); THREAD; PEN

Bethany wanted me to take her grad pictures. It was a bit intimidating, but we had so much fun trying to get the perfect shot! I think all 238 of them are perfect, but I am a bit biased!

BETHANY ANN

Sharon Laakkonen,
Superior, Wisconsin

With such quick and cool results, you won't be able to resist trying this rub-on and resist border technique. For a soft, yet girly border treatment for her daughter's graduation photo, Sharon applied white rub-on letters and a scrolly design. Using a sponge brush, she haphazardly dabbed on green and blue acrylic paints around the photo's border and over the rub-ons for a splash of color. She then rubbed the paint off of the rub-ons, revealing their white feminine designs.

SUPPLIES: PATTERNED PAPER (AUTUMN LEAVES); FOAM STAMPS (LI'L DAVIS DESIGNS); STICKER LETTERS (SEI); PLASTIC LETTERS (HEIDI SWAPP); PAINTS (MAKING MEMORIES); COLORED MARKERS; STAMPING INK

PETTING ZOO

Suzy Plantamura,
Laguna Niguel,
California

Zoom in on your photo subject or unify a photo montage with this painting technique. Suzy had several photos from a trip to a zoo, but their backgrounds clashed with one another and stole the limelight from the photos' subjects. To remedy this, Suzy brushed acrylic paint from the edges of the photos right up to each creature, highlighting them as the photo stars. The paint not only highlights each animal, but unifies them together on the page.

DANCE

Marie Cox,
Raleigh, North Carolina

Zoom in on a photo subject or hide unsightly background elements with a little paint and a masked design. Marie placed a floral mask over her photo. Then, using a paint-brush and pink acrylic paint, she stippled paint over the mask and onto the photo, silhouetting the photo subject. The painted frame brings focus directly to the photo star with her skirt carrying a transparency printed title.

SUPPLIES: CARDSTOCK; PINK PAINT, FLOWER MASK (HEIDI SWAPP); RUB-ONS (SCRAPWORKS); STICKERS (K & COMPANY); TRANSPARENCY (DAISY D'S)

WATERCOLOR PAINT

SUPPLIES: PATTERNED PAPER (BASIC GREY); BUTTONS (AUTUMN LEAVES); TRANSPARENCY, RUB-ONS (CREATIVE IMAGINATIONS); CANVAS PAPER (BLUMENTHAL CRAFT); WATERCOLORS (LOEW CORNELL); ADHESIVE

MOMENT

Shannon Taylor,
Bristol, Tennessee

You don't have to be a Monet or Renòir to paint a canvas masterpiece. No, with a canvas printed photo and a little watercolor paints, you can turn an ordinary photo into an intriguing work of art. Shannon printed the black-and-white photo of her son onto a canvas sheet and then frayed the edges by hand for a vintage look. With a paintbrush and watercolors, Shannon carefully painted the photo background, leaving her son's image black-and-white to highlight him. To retain photo details, use light colors and a sheer coat of paint.

SUPPLIES: PATTERNED PAPER (7 GYPSIES, DAISY D'S, SCENIC ROUTE PAPER CO.); TRANSPARENCY, TAB (KAREN RUSSELL); TEXTURED PAPER (FIBERMARK); GOLF LEAF PAINT (PLAID); GEL MEDIUM; THREAD; PEN

50

Deb Perry,
Newport News, Virginia

Highlight a focal photo with a dimensional gel-medium frame created directly on the photo. Deb applied layers of gel medium to the edges of her photo with a straight edge spatula, building up lots of texture. After the gel medium completely dried, she colored and enhanced the textured frame with a gold leaf pen, and then created a delicate scroll design on the photo's bottom righthand corner.

STEP ONE

Using a straight edge (knife or credit card), load a small amount of gel medium onto edges of photo with a swipe. This creates a random texture. Allow to dry.

STEP TWO

After gel medium is firm to touch, use gold leaf paint and a small paint brush to cover raised edges of photo.

The conditions in the ocean prevented us from really spending much time in the water this trip, but we did walk along the beach and hunt for shells quite a bit. This particular morning we were headed toward the public beach and the pier to see if anything exciting was happening. As we were walking under the pier, I stopped for just a moment to look down towards the end. The waves were crashing onto the shore and the way the pillars visually funnelled your eyes to the end of the pier was just stunning. It was so amazing. I had to take a picture. I love moments like this...moments when you come across something truly unexpected, and you can stop and take a second to really enjoy it.

A PERFECT MOMENT   A PERFECT MOMENT   A PERFECT MOMENT   A PERFE RFECT MOMENT

The Pier In Palm Beach, Florida

Spring Break March 2004

SUPPLIES: PATTERNED PAPER (SCENIC ROUTE PAPER CO.); METAL TAG (MAKING MEMORIES); EMBOSSING POWDER (PSX DESIGN); RIBBON (MAY ARTS); CARDSTOCK; ARIAL FONT (MICROSOFT)

A PERFECT MOMENT

Nicole Cholet,
Beaconsfield,
Quebec, Canada

Create a photo illusion with this altering technique. The tumultuous waves in this photo seem to splash onto the photo's edges. To create the water illusion, Nicole sanded the edges of the photo to expose some of the white background to appear like white caps. She then inked the photo's edges with shades of blue and green embossing ink. Clear embossing powder sprinkled onto the ink and then heat embossed creates a wet look reflective of the splashing waves.

TAKE NOTE *For further definition, sprinkle white embossing powder to the very edge of the photo and then heat emboss.*

EMBOSSING INK

4 ❤ DOZEN

Anniversaries have never been a really big deal for Neil and I. We usually just get a sitter for the evening and go out for dinner-nothing fancy… But not this year. My heart melted the moment I opened the door. I couldn't even see the delivery boy through all the flowers and balloons. There were 48 of these beautiful roses spilling out of the vase. Each one just as perfect as the others. After 11 years of marriage, Neil can still surprise me.

SUPPLIES: PATTERNED PAPER (CREATIVE IMAGINATIONS); LETTER STICKERS (PROVO CRAFT); CIRCLE STICKERS (7 GYPSIES); HEART SHAPE (ARTIST'S OWN DESIGN); STAMPING INK; WHITE EMBOSSING INK; BOOKMAN OLD STYLE FONT (MICROSOFT)

4 DOZEN

Nicole Cholet,
Beaconsfield, Quebec, Canada

Like a blur filter in image-editing software that softens a photo, this fast and fresh framing technique achieves the same dreamy effect but in half the time of a computer-generated manipulation. Nicole used a dauber to dab white embossing ink onto the photo's edges, applying it more heavily at the outer edges. As she moved toward the center, she applied less ink, creating the blurred effect. Try this technique to draw focus to a photo subject or to blur out any distracting elements.

SOLVENT INK

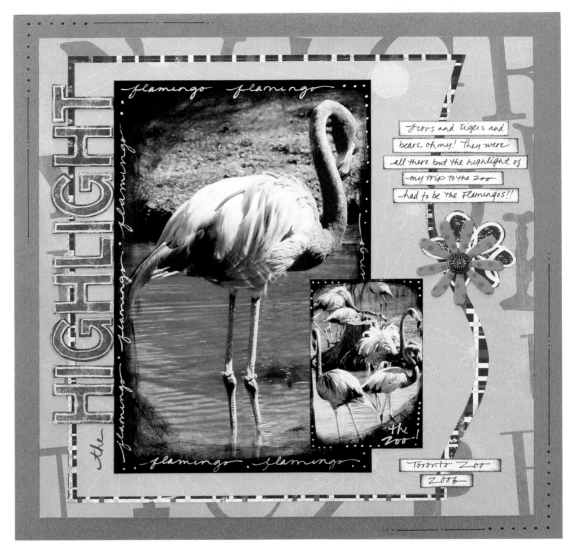

SUPPLIES: PATTERNED PAPER (IMAGINATION PROJECT, JUNKITZ); CHIPBOARD ACCENTS (IMAGINATION PROJECT); SOLVENT INK; DECORATIVE BRAD (MAKING MEMORIES); PEN; CARDSTOCK

THE HIGHLIGHT

Vicki Boutin,
Burlington, Ontario, Canada

To make a quick and custom frame all you need is an ink pad and a little dexterity. Vicki rubbed the edges of her photos with a solvent ink pad in a contrasting black that really makes the pink flamingoes in her photos pop. While the altered edges zoom in on magnificent creatures, it is also a great way to conceal a distracting background. To further customize the frame, Vicki journaled and doodled on the dried inked edges with a white gel pen for a whimsical effect.

Photo shoot: Baby in a bucket

caution: baby may try to eat her way out of the bucket while attempting to escape! H 127 06

REMEMBER

PHOTO SHOOT: BABY IN A BUCKET

Joanna Bolick, Fletcher, North Carolina

Create a quick photo title with this stamping technique. Joanna brushed an inkpad onto the edges of the photos for bold defining borders. With letter stamps and stamping ink, Joanna stamped her title onto the photos, starting the sentence on one photo and ending it on the other. This titling technique ties the photos together and adds continuity to the page. Use this trick to fill in empty real estate on the page.

SUPPLIES: PATTERNED PAPER (CREATIVE IMAGINATIONS, DAISY D'S, MAKING MEMORIES, MY MIND'S EYE); LETTER STAMPS (MAKING MEMORIES); DISTRESS INK; STAMPING INK

ONE LI'L BABY

Holly Corbett, Central, South Carolina

Use a touch of color to add meaning and life to a photo. Strewn baby socks may seem just that on the living room floor, but capture them in a black-and-white photo with a touch of blue, and the image comes to life as a heart-warming reminder of baby-boy feet. Holly printed the image onto photo paper with a luster finish. She dabbed the sweet socks lightly with stamping ink, using a cotton swab. The hand coloring adds a touch of meaning and sentiment to the still-life shot.

SUPPLIES: BRASS STENCIL (LASTING IMPRESSIONS); SANDPAPER; FLOWERS (PRIMA); LETTER STICKERS (BASIC GREY); CIRCLE LETTERS (LI'L DAVIS DESIGNS); "XOXO" CHARM, THREAD, "PRICELESS" BRAD, RHINESTONE BRADS (MAKING MEMORIES); CHIPBOARD LETTERS, HEART (HEIDI SWAPP); RIBBON (OFFRAY), STAMPING INK; CARDSTOCK

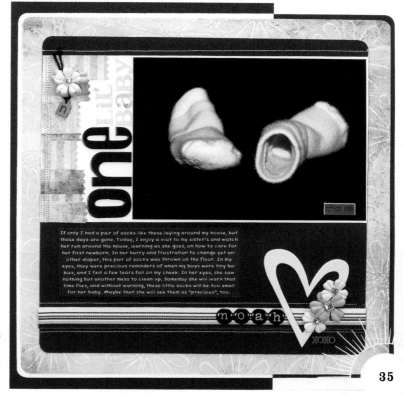

If only I had a pair of socks like these laying around my house, but those days are gone. Today, I enjoy a visit to my sister's and watch her run around the house, learning as she goes, on how to care for her first newborn. In her hurry and frustration to change yet another diaper, this pair of socks was thrown on the floor. In my eyes, they were precious reminders of when my boys were tiny babies, and I felt a few tears fall on my cheek. In her eyes, she saw nothing but another mess to clean up. Someday she will learn that time flies, and without warning, these little socks will be too small for her baby. Maybe then she will see them as "precious", too.

ALCOHOL INK

THE TWO OF YOU

Greta Hammond,
Goshen, Indiana

Add a touch of sheer color and design to your photos with this artsy yet easy technique. Greta mixed two custom colorants by combining clear gloss medium with pink and then green alcohol ink. She brushed on a sheer green border around the edges of the photo, and then applied the pink gloss to a daisy foam stamp and stamped onto the photo. The transparent wash of color adds a punch of color and yet allows the photo image to shine through.

SUPPLIES: PATTERNED PAPER (IMAGINATION PROJECT); RUB-ONS (7 GYPSIES, IMAGINATION PROJECT); CHIPBOARD LETTERS, FLOWER STAMP (HEIDI SWAPP); CHIPBOARD (IMAGINATION PROJECT); DIAMOND GLAZE (JUDIKINS); PHOTO TURN (BASIC GREY); ALCOHOL INKS (RANGER); BUTTONS (AUTUMN LEAVES); CARDSTOCK

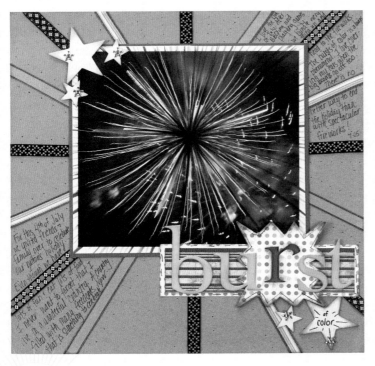

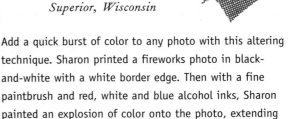

BURST OF COLOR

Sharon Laakkonen,
Superior, Wisconsin

Add a quick burst of color to any photo with this altering technique. Sharon printed a fireworks photo in black-and-white with a white border edge. Then with a fine paintbrush and red, white and blue alcohol inks, Sharon painted an explosion of color onto the photo, extending her lines onto the photo's white edge. Try this technique to boost the color on a color-printed photo as well.

SUPPLIES: PATTERNED PAPER (KI MEMORIES, SCENIC ROUTE PAPER CO.); RIBBON (PRIMA); CHIPBOARD ACCENTS (HEIDI SWAPP); STAMPING INK; ALCOHOL INKS (RANGER); HOLE POKER; BLACK PEN

SUPPLIES: PATTERNED PAPER (A2Z ESSENTIALS); CHIPBOARD FLOWERS (IMAGINATION PROJECT); RUB-ONS (7 GYPSIES, IMAGINATION PROJECT); BRADS (MAGIC SCRAPS); LETTER STICKERS (AMERICAN CRAFTS, CREATIVE IMAGINATIONS, DIE CUTS WITH A VIEW, SONNETS, STICKER STUDIO); BOTTLED DYE INK (RANGER); PEN; CARDSTOCK

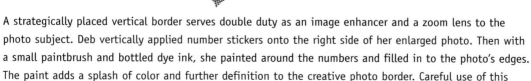

BIG GIRL

Deb Perry,
Newport News, Virginia

A strategically placed vertical border serves double duty as an image enhancer and a zoom lens to the photo subject. Deb vertically applied number stickers onto the right side of her enlarged photo. Then with a small paintbrush and bottled dye ink, she painted around the numbers and filled in to the photo's edges. The paint adds a splash of color and further definition to the creative photo border. Careful use of this altering technique plunges a photo subject into the limelight rather than stealing the show.

WATERCOLOR PENCILS

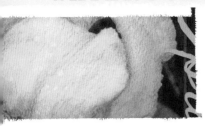

Spring

*The paintbrush of spring
Washes awakening life
With wild abandon*

SUPPLIES: WATERCOLOR PAPER
(STRATHMORE); WATERCOLOR PENCILS;
RIBBON (OFFRAY); FOAM SPACERS;
IMAGE EDITING SOFTWARE (ADOBE);
CARDSTOCK; LAMBO TITLE FONT

SPRING

*Torrey Scott,
Thornton, Colorado*

A photo printed on textural watercolor paper begs to be enhanced with the soft painterly touch of watercolor pencils. Combine these tools and techniques to turn a photo into museum-worthy art. With image-editing software, Torrey cropped in tightly on her iris photo subjects and then converted the images to black-and-white. She printed the photos onto watercolor paper, and then colored the images with watercolor pencils. With a paintbrush and water, Torrey blended the colored pencil. The water altered the black areas of the photo, creating the look of an authentic watercolor painting.

SUPPLIES: PATTERNED PAPER (AUTUMN LEAVES, KI MEMORIES); EPOXY STICKERS (AUTUMN LEAVES); WHITE PEN; COLORED MARKERS; CARDSTOCK

MY SPIRITED CHILD

Danielle Thompson,
Tucker, Georgia

Elements hand-drawn directly on a photo with permanent markers can add meaning and customize a photo. Hinting at her son's spirited personality, Danielle framed his photos with whimsically hand-drawn doodles directly on the photo. The doodles contour the child's face, drawing attention to the photos' subject and filling in the empty backgrounds. Scrolly handwritten descriptive words add further fun and meaning to the photos.

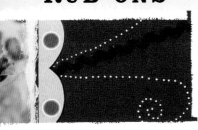

RUB-ONS

After a long winter, nature begins to renew itself with a magnificent display of color. Our yard is filled with early blooms to help jolt us into the coming season. I love the explosion of color and the possibilities it brings. Just the push I need to start fresh and new again.

SUPPLIES: PATTERNED PAPER (IMAGINATION PROJECT, SCENIC ROUTE PAPER CO.); BUTTERFLY RUB-ONS (BASIC GREY); DISTRESSED RUB-ONS (MY MIND'S EYE); BUTTON, RIBBON (MAKING MEMORIES); DIE-CUT FLOWER (SOURCE UNKNOWN); RICKRACK; WHITE PEN; CARDSTOCK

SPRING

Greta Hammond,
Goshen, Indiana

With the snappy application of rub-ons, you can put a dreamy, blurred filter onto photos in no time. To zoom in softly on her lovely flower garden, Greta applied distressed white rub-ons over the image with a wooden stick, overlapping the design onto the background paper. The distressed rub-ons have a subtle white-wash effect that softly frames and zooms in on the floral subjects.

SUPPLIES: PATTERNED PAPER
(K & COMPANY); CHIPBOARD
LETTERS AND ACCENTS (LI'L
DAVIS DESIGNS); FLOWER
STICKERS (TARGET); SEQUINS;
BRADS; CARDSTOCK

DEPARTED

Linda Harrison,
Sarasota, Florida

Subtly enhance or add a statement of sparkle to photo elements by hand coloring them with metallic rub-ons. Linda added instant glow to her portrait by applying green metallic rub-ons with a cotton swab to her shirt and then gently buffing it for a subdued highlight. A bronze tone swabbed on her face is gently blended for a touch of vibrancy. A concentrated wash of gold on her hat creates more obvious highlights. Vary the focus by varying the application and blending of the metallic colorant.

CHALK

TAKE NOTE *Prior to applying colorant, spray your image a matte finish to give it texture.*

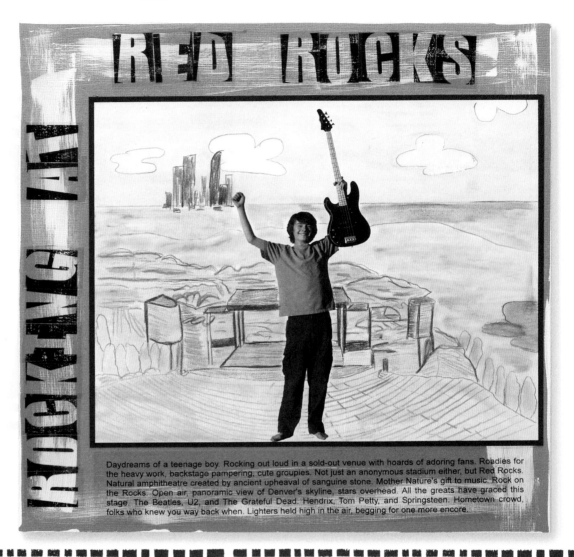

ROCKING AT RED ROCKS

Daydreams of a teenage boy. Rocking out loud in a sold-out venue with hoards of adoring fans. Roadies for the heavy work, backstage pampering, cute groupies. Not just an anonymous stadium either, but Red Rocks. Natural amphitheatre created by ancient upheaval of sanguine stone. Mother Nature's gift to music. Rock on the Rocks. Open air, panoramic view of Denver's skyline, stars overhead. All the greats have graced this stage. The Beatles, U2, and The Grateful Dead. Hendrix, Tom Petty, and Springsteen. Hometown crowd, folks who knew you way back when. Lighters held high in the air, begging for one more encore.

SUPPLIES: TRANSPARENCY
LETTERS (ADORN IT); CHALK
PENCIL (CHARTPAK); CHALK;
ACRYLIC PAINT; MATTE FINISH
SPRAY; CARDSTOCK

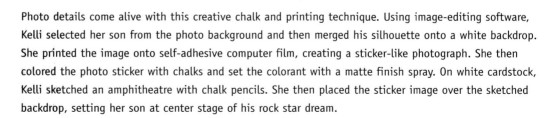

ROCKING AT RED ROCKS

Kelli Noto,
Centennial, Colorado

Photo details come alive with this creative chalk and printing technique. Using image-editing software, Kelli selected her son from the photo background and then merged his silhouette onto a white backdrop. She printed the image onto self-adhesive computer film, creating a sticker-like photograph. She then colored the photo sticker with chalks and set the colorant with a matte finish spray. On white cardstock, Kelli sketched an amphitheatre with chalk pencils. She then placed the sticker image over the sketched backdrop, setting her son at center stage of his rock star dream.

SANDING

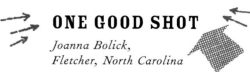

happiness

happy

being me

12.25.05

it only took
231 photos
of you (roughly)
to get this
good shot!

despite this fact I do believe you
are happier than you've ever been!

happy

happiness

happ

ONE GOOD SHOT

Joanna Bolick,
Fletcher, North Carolina

Try this subtle distressed effect to quickly frame
a photo or to disguise a background. Joanna
sanded the edges of a photo with sandpaper.
She then lightly brushed on acrylic paint with
a dry foam brush. The dash of paint softly
frames the black-and-white photo and draws
focus to the photo subject. A rub-on phrase
and design directly on the photo add a touch
of color and sentiment.

SUPPLIES: PATTERNED PAPER (BASIC GREY, CREATIVE IMAGINATIONS, MOD); SANDPAPER;
RUB-ONS (MOD); CARDSTOCK STICKERS (MAKING MEMORIES); LETTER RUB-ONS (HEIDI SWAPP);
ACRYLIC PAINT; STAPLES; BLACK PEN; MACHINE STITCHING; CARDSTOCK

MAYBE

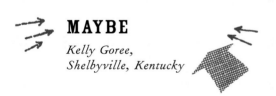

Kelly Goree,
Shelbyville, Kentucky

Like a favorite shirt softened and worn, sandpaper
can lend that same familiar and loved feel to your
photos. Kelly sanded the edges of her black-and-
white photos firmly with sandpaper, leaving a
softly distressed border. For further softness,
she rounded the corners of the photos with a
punch. She nestled them together for a snuggly
look, adhering the center photo slightly over the
others with dimensional adhesive.

and just
maybe.

It's because it's always been just the
two of us... or maybe it's because
you're the baby of the family... or
maybe it's simply because we're
so much alike. But whatever it is,
you're Mama's boy and I love it!

april 22, 2006
Mama & Carson

POLO

SUPPLIES: PATTERNED PAPER (CHERRY ARTE); PLASTIC
LETTERS (HEIDI SWAPP); SANDPAPER; PEN; CARDSTOCK

BLEACH STAMPING

SUPPLIES: TEXTURED
CARDSTOCK (PRISM); DESIGN
STAMPS (INKADINKADO,
STAMPA ROSA); LETTER STAMPS
(MA VINCI RELIQUARY); BLEACH
PEN; BRADS; FOAM SQUARES;
TRANSPARENCY

 ## SICILY

Torrey Scott,
Thornton, Colorado

Bleach stamping alters a photo in a way that leaves a grand impression. Try this technique to add
interest and an old world look to your photos. Torrey printed her photos onto white textured cardstock.
She applied gel bleach to architectural and letter stamps with her fingers. She then firmly stamped onto
the photos. The bleach ate away the photo's emulsion, leaving a slightly blurred impression. Stamps
with large raised portions and bold details work best to leave the greatest imprint. A column-stamped
background adds further interest, echoing the photos' architectural theme.

TAKE NOTE *You will achieve different results with a bleach pen on a processed photo, leaving colored streaks as opposed to the bluish-white lines on this black-and-white, inkjet-printed photo.*

SUPPLIES: PATTERNED PAPER (MY MIND'S EYE); CHIPBOARD LETTERS (LI'L DAVIS DESIGNS); RHINESTONE BRADS, SILVER BRADS (MAKING MEMORIES); RHINESTONE FLOWERS (SCRAPTIVITY); RHINESTONES (WESTRIM); RUB-ONS (KI MEMORIES); ACRYLIC FLOWERS, PHOTOTURNS (QUEEN & CO.); BLEACH PEN; PEN; CARDSTOCK

GLOW

*Vicki Boutin,
Burlington,
Ontario, Canada*

For an ultra edgy way to alter a photo, reach for a bleach pen. Vicki doodled a scroll and floral design by using the fine tip and brush end of a bleach pen directly on her photo. After three minutes, she rinsed the bleach from the photo, and allowed it to dry. The bleach worked like an eraser, removing the ink and leaving her with a glowing design. Try this cool technique to erase away a distracting background while adding a touch of art to your photos.

BLEACH DIPPING

SUPPLIES: CIRCLE FOAM STAMP (JUNKITZ); VELVET LETTERS (MAKING MEMORIES); RHINESTONES (BEADERY); CHIPBOARD ACCENTS (FANCY PANTS DESIGNS); EMBOSSED FELT (FOSS); BLACK PEN; BLEACH; ADHESIVE

CAROUSEL

Shannon Taylor,
Bristol, Tennessee

Lend a nostalgic touch to any photo with bleach dipping. Shannon used this technique to achieve a faded batik-like finish to her photo without the mess and trouble of melting wax. Since each photo will fade with different results, it is best to keep a close eye on the bleaching process.

STEP ONE

In a large bowl, dilute 1 ounce of bleach with 7 ounces of water. Fill another large bowl with water only. Place photo into bleach solution for 10-15 seconds. Photo will begin to fade and change color.

STEP TWO

Remove quickly and dip into water bowl to set. Hang to dry.

Timeless at THREE

Turner - at three years old, you are a true bundle of energy, always on the move. There is such a timeless quality to these photographs. I love that you were captured in your element - timeless at 3 - June 18, 2005

SUPPLIES: PATTERNED PAPER (SEI); LARGE CHIPBOARD LETTER (PRESSED PETALS); CHIPBOARD LETTERS, PHOTO CORNERS (HEIDI SWAPP); CIRCLE PUNCH; DIE-CUT FLOWERS (SOURCE UNKNOWN); BLEACH; STAMPING INK; PEN; CARDSTOCK

TIMELESS AT THREE

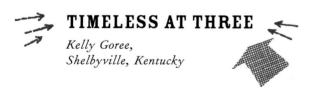

Kelly Goree,
Shelbyville, Kentucky

Kelly also used a wash of bleach to lend an antique look to a series of photos. The timeless **quality** worked great for her page theme, which she then played upon in her design and color scheme. **Try** the bleach dipping technique to soften clashing colors or to unify a photomontage.

EMBOSSING POWDER

Oh, yeah...that's you... Mr. Cool. Except when you aren't. I love that you are mostly always calm... and I love that when you're not, I know how to handle you. I love that when you start to stress, you rely on me. I love that you always return the favor. In your job, there is stress - worry that everything will go off without a hitch. And when you can't handle the pressure or you start to get a little on the crazy side, it's my role to come in and calm you down. I like being your wingman, your sidekick. I like keeping you from having a meltdown. We've got this thing down to a science by now. I love that about us.

SUPPLIES: PATTERNED PAPER, RIBBON (CHATTERBOX); CHIPBOARD LETTERS, LETTER SILHOUETTE (HEIDI SWAPP); LETTER STICKERS (AMERICAN CRAFTS); EMBOSSING INK; ULTRA THICK EMBOSSING POWDER; EMBROIDERY FLOSS; CARDSTOCK

CALM, COOL AND COLLECTED

Courtney Walsh,
Winnebago, Illinois

Create a crackle finish over your photo as an interesting filter and to add meaning to a photo subject. Courtney coated her husband's photo with clear embossing ink and then sprinkled it with ultra thick embossing powder. After melting the embossing powder with a heat tool, she repeated the process three times to achieve a very thick coating over the photo. She gently bent the photo back and forth, creating cracks in the embossed filter.

TAKE NOTE *To add dimension and a distressed feel, dab brown stamping ink onto the textured border.*

SUPPLIES: PATTERNED PAPER (IMAGINATION PROJECT, WE R MEMORY KEEPERS); CHIPBOARD LETTERS (HEIDI SWAPP); CHIPBOARD DESIGNS (FANCY PANTS DESIGNS); BUTTONS (AUTUMN LEAVES); LETTER STAMPS (PSX DESIGN); TAG (7 GYPSIES); EMBOSSING POWDER; EMBOSSING INK; STAMPING INK; CARDSTOCK

BALANCING LIFE

*Greta Hammond,
Goshen, Indiana*

Add a rustic look to photos with this printing and distressing technique. Greta printed her horse photo onto tan cardstock, leaving a ¼" (.64cm) border. She applied clear embossing ink to the edges, letting it randomly run onto the border. A sprinkling of heat set ultra thick embossing powder was repeated several times to create a dimensional rough border.

TISSUE PAPER

TAKE NOTE *Outline tissue paper pieces with black and white pens for further definition.*

SUPPLIES: CARDSTOCK; CHIPBOARD LETTERS (IMAGINATION PROJECT); LETTERS (K & COMPANY); GEL PEN; TISSUE PAPER; GEL MEDIUM; PEN

MERRY GO ROUND

*Deb Perry,
Newport News, Virginia*

Make a photo element pop with this creative enhancing technique. To add to the magic of a carousel horse, Deb traced its intricate details onto colored tissue paper and then cut out the pieces. She adhered the tissue paper cutouts onto the photo with gel medium, and then allowed it to dry. Deb completed the look by using the same technique on other photo and page elements.

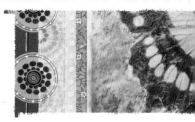

BUTTERFLY

*Vicki Boutin,
Burlington,
Ontario, Canada*

Tissue paper and colorant turn beautiful imagery into breathtaking artwork. Vicki sprayed her inkjet-printed butterfly photo with a fixative, and allowed it to dry. She then adhered torn tissue paper on top of the image with a matte gel medium. After adhering three layers of torn tissue paper, Vicki added a top coat of gel medium, and then let it dry overnight. Once dry, she enhanced the image by dabbing it with ink applied with cotton swabs and trimming the excess tissue from the photo's edge. The result is a textural photo with a very artsy feel.

SUPPLIES: PATTERNED PAPER (AUTUMN LEAVES, SANDYLION); STAMPS (SCRAPTIVITY); BRADS (QUEEN & CO.); STICKERS (IMAGINATION PROJECT); CHIPBOARD BOOKPLATE (BASIC GREY); FIXATIVE SPRAY; MATTE MEDIUM (LIQUITEX); STAMPING INK; PEN; CARDSTOCK

DISCOVER PARADISE

*Suzy Plantamura,
Laguna Niguel, California*

Turn any photo into a soft watercolor with this creative filter technique. Suzy covered a colorful landscape photo with a coat of gel medium. She layered small pieces of torn tissue paper over the photo onto the gel. A final coat of gel medium sealed the tissues. Once dry, Suzy colored the tissue collage with water-based markers that she smeared with her fingertips. A fine-tip black permanent marker outlined photo details, making them pop from the colorful collage.

SUPPLIES: PATTERNED PAPER (ADORN IT, K & COMPANY); RUB-ON LETTERS (AUTUMN LEAVES); RUB-ON ACCENTS (7 GYPSIES, K & COMPANY, MY MIND'S EYE); EPOXY STAMP (K & COMPANY); TISSUE PAPER; BLACK MARKER; GLOSS GEL MEDIUM (LIQUITEX); COLORED MARKERS; STAMPING INK

CRACKLE TECHNIQUE

TAKE NOTE *Use this crackle-finish framing technique to also add a vintage touch to photos.*

Adam has always been one to jump right in and get busy with things. It was no different on our vacation to our new favorite destination: the Turks & Caico's Islands. You put the gorgeous sands to immediate use!
10.2005

aDam

SUPPLIES: PATTERNED PAPER (SCENIC ROUTE PAPER CO., SEI); DIE-CUTS (QUICKUTZ); STICKERS (SEI); STAMPING INK; CRACKLE MEDIUM; ACRYLIC PAINT; CRAFT BEACH GLASS (SOURCE UNKNOWN); PEN; FOAM SQUARES; CARDSTOCK

HE'LL BUILD AN ISLAND

*Linda Harrison,
Sarasota, Florida*

Frame a photo in texture and color with this creative painting technique. Linda printed an 8" x 10" (20cm x 25cm) photo in the center of an 8½" x 11" (22cm x 28cm) sheet of photo paper, leaving a white border. With a paintbrush, she applied crackle medium to the white border and allowed it to dry until slightly tacky. She then brushed a coat of acrylic paint in long, even strokes over the crackle medium. Beach glass borders the photo, playing up the water effect created by the rippled paint.

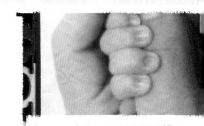

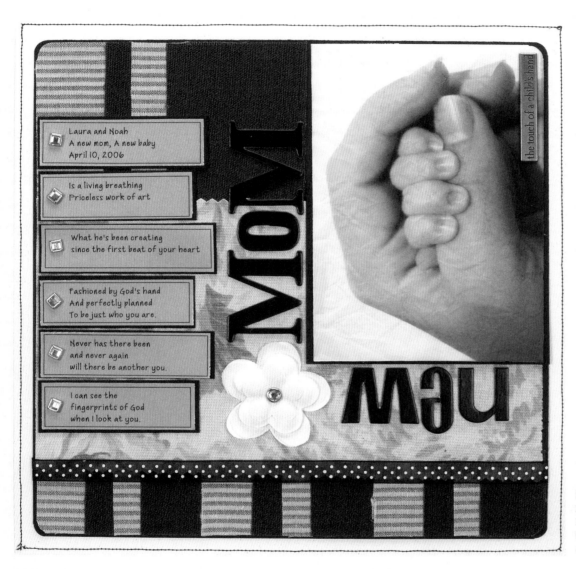

Laura and Noah
A new mom, A new baby
April 10, 2006

Is a living breathing
Priceless work of art

What he's been creating
since the first beat of your heart

Fashioned by God's hand
And perfectly planned
To be just who you are.

Never has there been
and never again
will there be another you.

I can see the
fingerprints of God
when I look at you.

Mom

new

the touch of a child's hand

SUPPLIES: FABRIC, FLOWER, BRADS, METAL PHRASE (MAKING MEMORIES); CHIPBOARD LETTERS (HEIDI SWAPP); RIBBON (MAY ARTS); VELLUM; CARDSTOCK

NEW MOM

Holly Corbett,
Central, South Carolina

Give any photo a heritage look with this faux crackling technique. Holly printed the black-and-white photo of her hand grasping her newborn's tiny fingers onto clear vellum. She then crumpled the photo to create the crackled-effect and flattened it with a warm iron. To echo the old fashioned feel, Holly matted the photo with a simple black mat surrounded by vintage-patterned fabrics.

HEAT TOOL ENGRAVING

TAKE NOTE *For best results with this technique, keep the tool moving to prevent burn marks.*

SUPPLIES: PATTERNED PAPER (BASIC GREY, DIE CUTS WITH A VIEW); DIE-CUT HEART, RUB-ON, SCROLL TEMPLATE (QUICKUTZ); HOT BOSS HEATING TOOL (ADORN IT); CARDSTOCK

FAMILY, '05

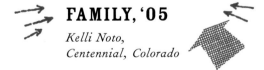

*Kelli Noto,
Centennial, Colorado*

Add an engraved design or a freehand doodle to your photos with this engraving technique. To add a touch of elegance to a black-and-white family portrait, Kelli used a die-cut template with a hot engraving tool to etch the scrolly border directly into the photo. The hot tool burned away the photo's emulsion, leaving a white etched design. To further customize her photo, Kelli etched a freehand title.

54

The wrought iron in Savannah is absolutely gorgeous. Many of the historic homes feature it on railings and iron basket holders. To me it is some of the most beautiful but over looked pieces of art ever created.

SUPPLIES: PATTERNED PAPER (BASIC GREY); FLORAL ACCENTS (PRIMA); BRADS (QUEEN & CO.); METAL ACCENTS (CLUB SCRAP, MICHAELS); ENGRAVING TOOL; DISTRESS INK; WHITE PEN; CARDSTOCK

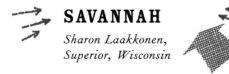

SAVANNAH

Sharon Laakkonen,
Superior, Wisconsin

Whether you want to highlight interesting architecture or bring out an intricate design, try this altering technique to call attention to any photo detail. Appreciating the handiwork of these vintage wrought-iron railings, Sharon emphasizes them by tracing their detail with a fine-tipped hot engraving tool. The engraver burns away the photo's emulsion, leaving an etched white design. Use this technique to emphasize an important element on any photo.

little treasures Love is memories he loves Absolutely

TOOT, TOOT!

*A BOY AND HIS TRAINS

extraordinary EMBELLISHMENTS

WHILE YOUR PHOTOS are most certainly works of art on their own, there's no harm in adding a dash of spice every now and again. Enter embellishments. You use them every day to give your layouts that extra punch of visual variety; now it's time to expand upon their versatility by using them directly on photos. The following chapter offers a sampling of layouts with embellished photos. Discover a treasure trove of ways to use titles, journaling, textiles, mesh, mica and more on your photos to make them pop right off the page!

Heather, you are so many things I wish I could be. :) You are laid back, you don't stress about the small things, you are an amazing mom, you laugh a lot, you aren't overly ambitious, you focus on just enjoying the moment, your life is about having fun, you exist slowly through life - never rushing things - always soaking it in, you're never in a hurry. I've learned a lot from Ethan and you, his sister, are no different. Thank you.

eat my dust

good times

I love that you are so caught up in your little world of make-believe.

& ......HAPPINE

ety of jewelry and as, you are almost always **DRESSED UP** as something yourself. But I love the imagination arks!

ow... you'll always be

cess in my book!

SS OPHIA

DISCOVER

RUB-ONS	DESIGN ELEMENTS
STAMPS	BAUBLES
DOODLES	TRANSPARENCY

RUB-ONS

SUPPLIES: PATTERNED PAPER
(BASIC GREY, MAKING MEMORIES,
PAPER SALON); RUB-ONS (ANNA GRIFFIN,
SCRAPPERWEAR); TRANSPARENCY
(HAMBLY STUDIOS); PHOTO TAB
(KAREN RUSSELL); SANDPAPER; PEN

GOING TO THE ZOO

*Joanna Bolick,
Fletcher, North Carolina*

Add instant interest and sentiment to a photo with rub-ons. With a wooden stick, Joanna applied
a mix of rub-on letters directly onto her photo to form the title and a rub-on design and sentiment
to tout the date. The rub-on title slightly overlap the background for a continuous feel while an
intricate transparency design encapsulating a whimsical rub-on elephant overlaps the focal photo
for a seamless look.

TAKE NOTE *For perfect positioning, use acrylic letters on a clear block to stamp the words.*

ISOLD'S
NEW
SHOES

I should have had a girl...maybe giving me three boys (and I feel that I should mention that they *are* wonderful boys) was God's way of keeping me from going into life long debt from buying all those adorable girls clothes and shoes. Let's be honest here, how could I possibly be expected to resist such adorable items? I suppose it's a good thing that Yvonne lets me gush over Isold and her new purchases. I can at least get it out of my system. I have to say that when I answered the door bell today and saw Isold at the door, dropping by to show me her new shoes, I actually got giddy! Show me those shoes, girly! What? You got two new pairs! How *cool* is that! She's a shoe freak just like me! I wasn't able to go on this shopping trip but I did get the full account of Isold strutting around the store trying to choose her favourite pair. Let's not forget that she's two and she's doing this. I really, really should have had a girl!

SUPPLIES: PATTERNED PAPER (SCENIC ROUTE PAPER CO.); STAMPS (TECHNIQUE TUESDAY); RIBBON (MAY ARTS); BRADS; STAMPING INK; CARDSTOCK; TAHOMA FONT (MICROSOFT)

ISOLD'S NEW SHOES

Nicole Cholet,
Beaconsfield,
Quebec, Canada

A title stamped directly onto a photo is so simple and yet can serve more purpose on a page than just titling it. As in this case, Nicole's photo-stamped title draws focus to the page subject and fills in an otherwise blank spot on the photo. The creative use of space frees up valuable page real estate to make room for other elements, such as an oversized photo, support photos and lots of journaling. The strategically stamped blue title creates a visual triangle with the other denim blue photo elements, balancing the page.

SUPPLIES: PATTERNED PAPER, CHIPBOARD ACCENTS, LETTER STICKERS (BASIC GREY); SNOWFLAKE (TARGET); STAMPING INK; PEN; CARDSTOCK

TAKE TIME TO CHASE THE SNOWFLAKES

Kelly Goree,
Shelbyville, Kentucky

Use a title to add visual interest and call out that special photo. Kelly created a photo collage with one enlarged focal photo and two smaller support photos. To draw attention to the focal photo, she spelled her title directly on it with a mix of cardstock letter stickers and handwritten words. A series of cardstock sticker dots draw the eye through the page.

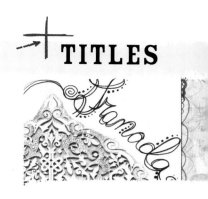

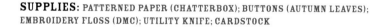

still feels like
HOME
to me...

It's not my home anymore. I don't live here on this beautiful piece of property in this sweet little town in this cozy home. I haven't quite figured out how my mom does it. How does she create this homey atmosphere? How can I make my house the kind of place my children really never want to leave? How can I make all of our visitors feel so comfortable in our house they kick their shoes off and stay awhile? My parents' house is one of my favorite places in the world. We go here when we need a break from reality. We go here to let the kids run like crazy, to wear themselves out on the big hill, to play like children should: with reckless abandon. We go to rest, to get rejuvenated. We never leave disappointed. I think everyone should have a place of escape... and for us... this is it. In so many ways, this will always be HOME to me.

SUPPLIES: PATTERNED PAPER (CHATTERBOX); BUTTONS (AUTUMN LEAVES); EMBROIDERY FLOSS (DMC); UTILITY KNIFE; CARDSTOCK

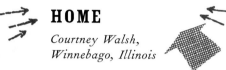

HOME

Courtney Walsh,
Winnebago, Illinois

A super-sized photo carrying a title of the same scale pops with this creative cutting technique. Using image-editing software, Courtney enlarged her photo and then layered it with white text in a cursive font. After printing the photo, she cut out large silhouetted letters from the photo, spelling "home." She matted the photo with red cardstock, causing the cutout letters to boldly standout.

GRANADA

Danielle Thompson,
Tucker, Georgia

Enhance a photo with a creative collage and a scripty handwritten title. Highlighting the beautiful architecture in this photo, Danielle used permanent markers to write a fancy title directly on it. A hand-drawn scalloped border frames the photos while butterflies handcut from patterned papers then mounted with dimensional adhesive flutter over the photo's edge. The collage adds an artsy flair to the photo.

SUPPLIES: PATTERNED PAPER (BASIC GREY, HAMBLY STUDIOS); BUTTONS (AUTUMN LEAVES); RUB-ON (DIE CUTS WITH A VIEW); MARKERS; PEN; EMBROIDERY FLOSS; FOAM TAPE

61

JOURNALING

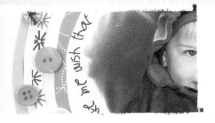

TAKE NOTE *If you're not computer savvy, try this same technique with a permanent pen and your own handwriting on the photo around a subject.*

SUPPLIES: PATTERNED PAPER (ADORN IT); DIE-CUT LETTERS (QUICKUTZ); FLUID CHALK INK; CARDSTOCK

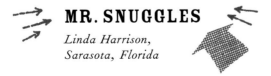

MR. SNUGGLES

Linda Harrison,
Sarasota, Florida

Silhouetting a subject with journaling text adds whimsy and a sense of movement to the photo. Linda first imported her photo into image-editing software. Then using the layers palette, she placed journaling text over the photo, silhouetting her son. A series of circle frames cut from cardstock and patterned paper zooms in on the subject and adds a further sense of action.

SUPPLIES: PATTERNED PAPER (HAMBLY STUDIOS, SASSAFRASS LASS); METAL PHOTO CORNER (MAKING MEMORIES); CHIPBOARD LETTERS (HEIDI SWAPP); LETTER STICKERS (AMERICAN CRAFT, K & COMPANY); MARKERS; EMBROIDERY FLOSS; WHITE PEN

HEATHER

Danielle Thompson,
Tucker, Georgia

Equipped with a permanent pen and a little creativity, you can customize any photo. Danielle handwrote her journaling directly onto the photo, wrapping the text around the silhouette of the photo subject. Beyond telling the story, the text highlights the photo subject as well as fills in space. Hand-drawn dots and decorative swirls on the background paper frame the photo with spunk. The customized design continued onto the title letters ties the photo to the page.

JOURNALING

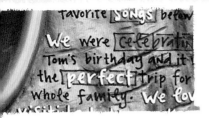

SUPPLIES: PATTERNED PAPER (BASIC GREY); CHIPBOARD LETTERS (LI'L DAVIS DESIGNS); LETTER STICKERS (EK SUCCESS); FLOWER (BAZZILL); BUTTONS (AUTUMN LEAVES); RIBBON (SOURCE UNKNOWN); EMBROIDERY FLOSS; WHITE GEL PEN; RED PEN; MARKERS; STAMPING INK

CALIFORNIA ADVENTURE LAND

Suzy Plantamura,
Laguna Niguel, California

Journaling printed directly onto the photo can help tell the story as well as enhance the photo subject. Suzy used a mix of permanent markers to journal directly onto the photo. Hand-drawn rectangles highlight key words while a shift in color emphasizes important phrases. Doodles add a touch of custom embellishment to the photo.

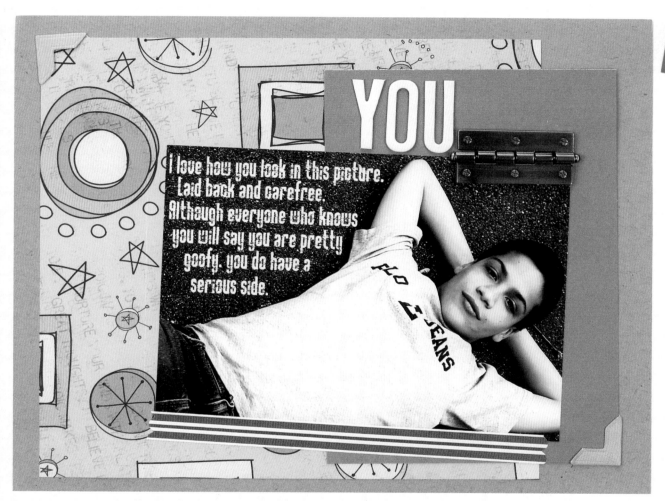

SUPPLIES: PATTERNED PAPER (AUTUMN LEAVES); METAL LATCH (7 GYPSIES); CHIPBOARD LETTERS, PHOTO CORNERS (HEIDI SWAPP); IMAGE EDITING SOFTWARE (ADOBE); CARDSTOCK

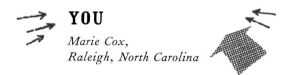

YOU

Marie Cox,
Raleigh, North Carolina

Journaling printed directly on an image serves dual purpose as a storyteller and a highlighter of the photo subject. With image-editing software, Marie changed her photo to black-and-white. Then using the layers palette, she created her journaling and placed it over the image before printing it. The text wraps around the silhouette of the photo subject while zooming in on him and filling in a blank background. The rugged and distressed font adds to the masculine page theme.

SUPPLIES: PATTERNED PAPER (KI MEMORIES); RUB-ON STITCHING (DIE CUTS WITH A VIEW); RHINESTONES (K & COMPANY, ME & MY BIG IDEAS); LETTER STAMPS (FONTWERKS, MAKING MEMORIES); WHITE MARKER (UNIBALL); COLORED PENS; COLORED MARKERS; CARDSTOCK

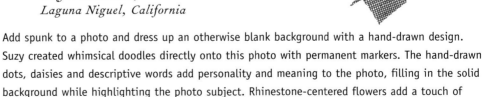

CHLOE LOVES TO PLAY PEEK-A-BOO

Suzy Plantamura,
Laguna Niguel, California

Add spunk to a photo and dress up an otherwise blank background with a hand-drawn design. Suzy created whimsical doodles directly onto this photo with permanent markers. The hand-drawn dots, daisies and descriptive words add personality and meaning to the photo, filling in the solid background while highlighting the photo subject. Rhinestone-centered flowers add a touch of sparkle and finish the playful design.

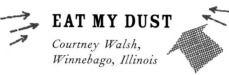

Watching Ethan on his "motorcycle,"
I was struck by the symbolism of this scene.
My little boy, gaining a bit more independence...
riding away from Mommy and Daddy to explore new lands.
Traveling in uncharted territory and becoming the little person
God intends for him to become. Somehow, I don't think I'm quite ready for this.
But everything in him is saying, "Eat my dust." It's pretty clear I don't have a choice!

SUPPLIES: PATTERNED PAPER (CHATTERBOX); PHOTO TURNS (7 GYPSIES); CHIPBOARD LETTERS (HEIDI SWAPP); BRADS; STAMPING INK; CIRCLE PUNCH; PEN; CARDSTOCK

EAT MY DUST

Courtney Walsh,
Winnebago, Illinois

Let your creative spirit flow with freehand photo doodling. Just like the days of scribbling on her notebook while daydreaming in class, Courtney used a permanent pen to draw whimsical scrolls and dots on this photo. While expressing her inner artist, the simple design enhances her chipboard title adhered directly on the photo and brings a meaningful sense of action to the photo.

A BOY AND HIS TRAINS

Danielle Thompson,
Tucker, Georgia

You don't have to be a precision artist to add a playful touch to your photos with hand-drawn elements. Using a fine-point ink pen, Danielle roughly sketched train tracks directly onto the photo for a childlike touch. The track adds movement to the image, drawing the eye across the photo. A thought bubble sketched with a broad tipped permanent marker adds a sense of fun. Danielle's handiwork continued onto the background pulls the photo and page together.

SUPPLIES: PATTERNED PAPER (AUTUMN LEAVES, KI MEMORIES); WORD STICKERS (K & COMPANY); RUB-ONS (AUTUMN LEAVES); CORNER ROUNDER; MARKERS; PEN; CARDSTOCK

SUPPLIES: PATTERNED PAPER (ANNA GRIFFIN, HAMBLY STUDIOS, KAREN RUSSELL); TRANSPARENCY (HAMBLY STUDIOS); STICKER (7 GYPSIES); CARDSTOCK

ALWAYS & FOREVER

Joanna Bolick,
Fletcher, North Carolina

Play up a photo element with this framing technique. Joanna trimmed the center out of a preprinted transparency and laid the circular design over the photo. The ring-like frame zooms in on the photo subject and also adds symbolism to the photo. Sticker sentiments and journaling strip layered over the transparency add further meaning and interest.

COSTUMED

Kelly Goree,
Shelbyville, Kentucky

To enhance an interesting photo element, repeat it with design details on the photo and throughout the page. To mimic the flames on her son's dragon costume, Kelly hand cut and silhouetted large patterned paper flames, and then matted them with orange cardstock. The flames flow over and behind her photos while being further ignited by a mix of scrolly rub-ons and freehand doodles.

SUPPLIES: PATTERNED PAPER (CHERRY ARTE); WOVEN LETTER TABS (SCRAPWORKS); RUB-ONS (BASIC GREY); STAMPING INK; PEN; CARDSTOCK

YOUR SHADOW

Greta Hammond,
Goshen, Indiana

A mix of computer-generated tricks along with hands-on scrapbooking techniques add dimensional design and interest to a photo. Greta first imported her photo into image-editing software. Using the layers palette, she applied a Gaussian Blur filter to the image for a dreamy, soft masking. Next, she applied a grunge mask to the photo's edges and colored the design black. A stamp and brush tool created the swirl and circle designs. After printing the photo, Greta further embellished her digital design with rub-ons and punched stars centered with brads.

SUPPLIES: PATTERNED PAPER (SCENIC ROUTE PAPER CO.); CHIPBOARD BRACKETS (HEIDI SWAPP); CHIPBOARD LETTERS (MAKING MEMORIES); CHIPBOARD FLOWER (IMAGINATION PROJECT); STAMPS (SCRAPTIVITY); PHOTO TURNS (7 GYPSIES); STAMPING INK; BROWN PEN; CARDSTOCK

TEXTILES

TAKE NOTE *Experiment with different stitches and mix embroidery floss colors for added interest to your photos.*

SUPPLIES: PATTERNED PAPER (BASIC GREY, CHATTERBOX, CRATE PAPER, IMAGINATION PROJECT); FLOWERS, RIBBON (PRIMA); BUTTONS (AUTUMN LEAVES); COASTER LETTERS (IMAGINATION PROJECT); EMBROIDERY THREAD (DMC); THREAD; DISTRESS INKS; FOAM SPACERS

SNUGGLER

*Sharon Laakkonen,
Superior, Wisconsin*

For a homespun touch and added texure, stitch a photo border. Sharon matted her photo onto cardstock, and then adhered it to the page with dimensional adhesive. Using a sewing needle and embroidery floss, she created a blanket stitch that pierced through the photo, around the mat's edge and through the background paper. The border adds textural coziness that plays on Sharon's page theme.

NO; they're not pigtails. Pigtails are braided... doggie ears aren't. If you were a member of my family, and you were a girl...you wore doggie ears. Mom and I sure look cute in our canine doos!

SUPPLIES: PATTERNED PAPER (JUNKITZ, PAPER STUDIO); STITCH STAMP (HERO ARTS); STAMPING INK; RIBBON (AMERICAN CRAFTS, OFFRAY); FLOWER TAG (MAKING MEMORIES); TRANSPARENCY; ACRYLIC PAINT; IMAGE EDITING SOFTWARE (ADOBE); CARDSTOCK; PLATFORM SHOES TITLE FONT (TWO PEAS IN A BUCKET)

DOGGIE EARS

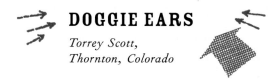

Torrey Scott,
Thornton, Colorado

A simple ribbon becomes a useful prop when added to a photo for a punch of personality. Ribbon can be used to emphasize a photo element or to create a colorful border. With image-editing software, Torrey removed the ribbons she and her mom were already sporting in their hair in the photos so they wouldn't detract from the real bows she soon added. She printed the black-and-white photos, cut a border of slits in each and then wove ribbon through the slits. Bows adhered on each photo highlight the hair dos and page theme—doggie ears.

SUPPLIES: PATTERNED
PAPER (FONTWERKS, LI'L
DAVIS DESIGNS, SANDYLION);
EMBROIDERY FLOSS; BUTTONS
(SOURCE UNKNOWN); WHITE
PEN; CARDSTOCK

YOU HAVE A PLACE IN MY HEART

Suzy Plantamura,
Laguna Niguel, California

Spotlight a photo element and add a touch of texture with this stitching technique. Following a chalked sidewalk heart on the photo, Suzy embroidered a straight stitch to highlight it. Embroidered letters directly on the photo create a homespun title.

[good times]

I love that you are so caught up in your little world of make-believe.

& ......HAPPINESS......

SUPPLIES: PATTERNED PAPER (MOD); CHIPBOARD ACCENTS (HEIDI SWAPP); RUB-ONS (K & COMPANY); EMBROIDERY FLOSS (MAKING MEMORIES); CARDSTOCK

GOOD TIMES

Marie Cox,
Raleigh, North Carolina

Something as simple and charming as hand stitching can call loads of attention to your photos. Using embroidery floss and a needle, Marie hand stitched a frame directly onto her black-and-white focal photo. A circle of stitches on the support photo zoom focus on her daughter's hands and toy.

My **5** year old princess

You are SUCH a *girly* girl.

With a wide variety of jewelry and feather boas, you are almost always

DRESSED UP as something other than yourself. But I love the imagination your play time sparks!

And just so you know... you'll always be

a princess in my book!

Princess
SOPHIA

SUPPLIES: PATTERNED PAPER (ARCTIC FROG, PROVO CRAFT); CHIPBOARD LETTERS (HEIDI SWAPP); BEADS (MICHAELS); DYE INK; CARDSTOCK; CENTURY GOTHIC BOLD, CLARENDON, BICKLEY SCRIPT FONTS

PRINCESS SOPHIA

Courtney Walsh,
Winnebago, Illinois

Put the spotlight on a special photo element with this embellishing technique. To truly adorn a crowned princess, Courtney outlined the crown's detailing in the photo with dimensional adhesive. She sprinkled pink micro beads onto the photo, shaking off the excess into a shoe box lid. Die-cut stars got the same bead-embellished royal treatment. Courtney finished by placing a few beads to fill in blank spots.

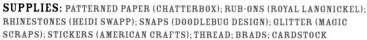

SUPPLIES: PATTERNED PAPER (CHATTERBOX); RUB-ONS (ROYAL LANGNICKEL); RHINESTONES (HEIDI SWAPP); SNAPS (DOODLEBUG DESIGN); GLITTER (MAGIC SCRAPS); STICKERS (AMERICAN CRAFTS); THREAD; BRADS; CARDSTOCK

DIVA IN TRAINING

Nicole Cholet,
Beaconsfield,
Quebec, Canada

Transcend your photos from ordinary to fabulous with a few distinctly placed baubles. To play up the intricate details of this jean jacket in the photo, Nicole followed the stitching lines with an application of glue and then sprinkled on blue glitter a for subtle accent. Strategically placed pink rhinestones add punch to the jacket's buttons and highlight the girl's hair with a touch of sparkle. Try this embellishing technique to add dimension and attention to any photo.

SPRINKLED

Kelly Goree,
Shelbyville, Kentucky

Bring a photo element to life with a resounding design choice. You can almost hear the splish-splash of water in this photo as Kelly plays up the wet theme. She sprinkled droplets of epoxy buttons across the photo and up the page, and highlighted a select few with a white paint pen. The repetition drives home the page theme while adding continuity throughout the page.

SUPPLIES: CARDSTOCK; DECORATIVE TAPES, PLASTIC LETTERS (HEIDI SWAPP); BUTTONS (DOODLEBUG DESIGN); WHITE PEN

METAL MESH

TAKE NOTE *Metal mesh works great to play up masculine themes.*

SUPPLIES: PATTERNED PAPER (KI MEMORIES); METAL MESH (MAKING MEMORIES); CHIPBOARD LETTERS (HEIDI SWAPP); CHIPBOARD ACCENTS (BASIC GREY); CORNER ROUNDER; CIRCLE CUTTER; CARDSTOCK

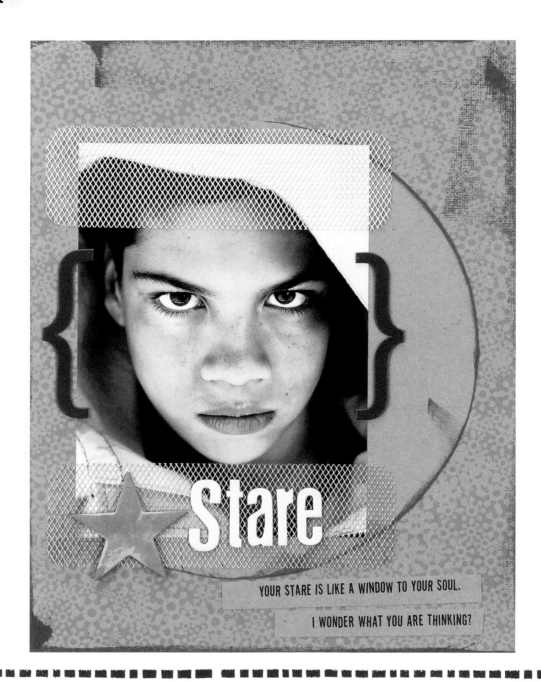

Stare

YOUR STARE IS LIKE A WINDOW TO YOUR SOUL.

I WONDER WHAT YOU ARE THINKING?

STARE

Marie Cox,
Raleigh, North Carolina

Whether you frame, border or completely overlay a photo with metal mesh, its fine weave provides a balance of covering mystique and revealing peek holes to allow your photo to shine through. To play up an intense stare, Marie bordered the top and bottom of this photo with wide strips of metal mesh. To slightly soften the look, she used a punch to round the corners of the metal borders.

POUNDING

 NIKI 2006

It starts out with a little twinge of pain in the back or side of my head. It's almost not even pain. It's just a throb but it doesn't take long for it to turn into so much more. On the worst days, it feels like my head is going to crack open and explode. I don't want to open my eyes, any noise is too loud, and my head hurts so bad, I just want to curl up and die. Logically I know that the pain will go away, but in middle of it, it seems like it's taking a lifetime for the medication to kick in. Sleeping is the only way to get through the worst of the pain. When it's just a headache, I get irritable, and my patience goes out the window. It's not real fair to the boys, but they are incredibly understanding, and I try to explain what is happening and why. It's actually pretty amazing how good they can be when they know I can't take any more.

I've suffered from headaches and migraines for as long as I can remember. It was difficult when I was younger. I had no idea what would bring the headaches on, and no idea how to get rid of them. I felt powerless. Over the years I've learned how to prevent many of them and what to do about the one's I can't. It is better now but I still dread the days when I wake up and my head is already pounding.

SUPPLIES: PATTERNED PAPER (MY MIND'S EYE); METAL TAG, PHOTO TURNS (MAKING MEMORIES); RIBBON (MAY ARTS, OFFRAY); STICKERS (PROVO CRAFT); MICA (US ARTQUEST); CENTURY GOTHIC FONT (MICROSOFT)

POUNDING

Nicole Cholet,
Beaconsfield,
Quebec, Canada

The smoky yet sheer quality of mica makes it a perfect photo filter. Its earthy brown tones lend a heritage feel and can enhance emotion in a photo. Nicole used layered mica to mimic shattered glass over her pain-evident portrait. To be sure to not cover too much of the image, she pulled the mica apart and used its thinnest layers. She adhered the fine sheets with vellum adhesive, overlapping the pieces to achieve the jagged effect. For a finished look, Nicole trimmed the mica from the edges of the photo.

77

TRANSPARENCY

SUPPLIES: CARDSTOCK;
TRANSPARENCY; DISTRESS
INK; PEN; LANE NARROW FONT

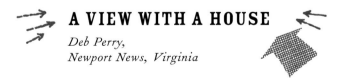

A VIEW WITH A HOUSE

Deb Perry,
Newport News, Virginia

The beauty of nature is almost too delicate to capture, but Deb did so perfectly on this layout
bursting with fall color. She started by printing a washed out photo onto regular photo paper.
She then printed the same photo onto a transparency after adding a few additional leaves in
image-editing software, and then trimmed the transparency to fit over the original photo. She took
the technique a step further by printing an image of the bench in a light tone on transparency,
and then enhancing it with bottled dye ink to achieve a golden watercolor effect that mimics the
setting sun in her smaller photo.

I love you so much it actually hurts sometimes

I think you are too darn cute! I am the luckiest Momma ever!

I am proud of you everyday. These things are 4 certain.

SUPPLIES: PATTERNED PAPER (IMAGINATION PROJECT); STAMPS (SCRAPTIVITY); BRAD, LETTER STICKERS (MAKING MEMORIES); DECORATIVE PAPERCLIPS (NUNN DESIGNS); IMAGE EDITING SOFTWARE (ADOBE); STARS (TWO PEAS IN A BUCKET); FIXATIVE SPRAY; TRANSPARENCY; STAR CLIP (SOURCE UNKNOWN); STAMPING INK; CARDSTOCK

4 CERTAIN

Vicki Boutin,
Burlington,
Ontario, Canada

A custom overlay can add just the right touch to a photo, playing up its unique theme. Vicki created a star and border design using computer brushes and image-editing software. She printed the design onto a transparency, and then set the printer ink with a fixative spray. She colored the stars with dye ink and cotton swabs, and then sprayed another coat of sealant. The whimsical design laid over the photo adds to the youthful spirit.

growing old
with you by my
side.
always
and
forever
we will be
together.

i love you!
Your loving wife,
Suzy
Happy Anniversar

8

GOOD
MEMORIES

love you more every day

sensational SURFACES

IT MAY SEEM HARD TO BELIEVE, but there are scores of artistic possibilities for printing photos besides standard photo paper. Don't be afraid to mix it up by trying new surfaces such as transparency and canvas. You'll also find the fun in experimenting with photo transfer techniques that use items already in your craft supply such as gel medium, packing tape or xylene blender pens. The options are endless and so is the fun! So get your creative groove on and discover new ways to produce photos with stunning effects.

get over it

OPERATING MANUAL
NOT INCLUDED

Cry if I put you in water, don't want

You have to just get o

Sweet DAY
f HopE joy
ughter &
LoVE
Aaron
&
Shannon
Feb 12
2006

And it's working!

y

february
march
april
may
june
july
august
september
october
november
december

GIRLY

I love Dooney & Bourke purses and

I love getting pedicures and wearin

I have more shoes then

I love getting my hair done a

I love laughing wi

just b

GIRL

DISCOVER:

→ TRANSPARENCY	→ GEL MEDIUM TRANSFER
→ CANVAS	→ LAZERTRAN TRANSFER
→ XYLENE PHOTO TRANSFER	→ IRON-ON TRANSFER

81

TRANSPARENCY

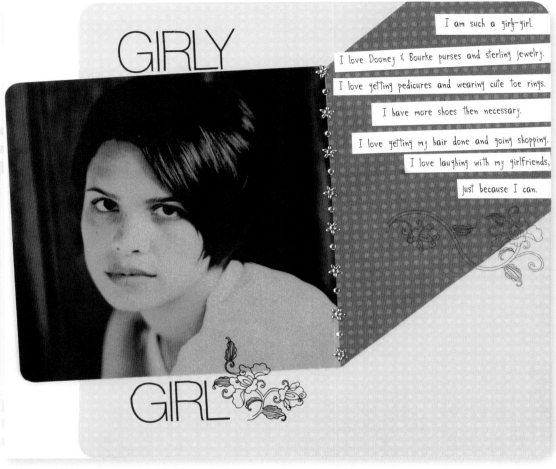

GIRLY

I am such a girly-girl.

I love Dooney & Bourke purses and sterling jewelry.

I love getting pedicures and wearing cute toe rings.

I have more shoes then necessary.

I love getting my hair done and going shopping.

I love laughing with my girlfriends,

just because I can.

GIRL

SUPPLIES: PATTERNED PAPER (KI MEMORIES); TRANSPARENCY; RUB-ON (AMERICAN CRAFTS, BASIC GREY); JEWELS (HEIDI SWAPP); CARDSTOCK; FRAPPACHINO FONT (TWO PEAS IN A BUCKET)

GIRLY GIRL

Marie Cox,
Raleigh, North Carolina

A photo printed on transparency becomes an instant overlay, inviting you to layer it on patterns and colors for added whimsy or meaning. Marie printed her black-and-white portrait onto a transparency sheet. To emphasize her page theme, she matted the transparency photo with pink cardstock for a girly look. Play with transparency photos and patterned papers for a collage look that's truly unique.

TAKE NOTE *To further highlight a transparency photo subject, try adding colorants such as alcohol inks.*

Every minute of every day…that is how often I strive to be happy.

It's totally impossible to be happy every single minute of your life…I am well aware.

There are things you just can't control.   But it IS possible to give it your best shot. And that's what I do.

I try and make every one of my moments the happiest it can be.

I do it for my friends.   For my family.

I do it for my husband.

I do it for my son.

And I do it for me.

And I do it to have the best life I can have. And it's working!

H A P P Y

Twenty-four seven.

SUPPLIES: PATTERNED PAPER (SCENIC ROUTE PAPER CO.); CALENDAR PAGE (KI MEMORIES); DATE STICKERS (EK SUCCESS); LETTER BUTTONS (JUNKITZ); BUTTONS (JO-ANN STORES); FLOWERS (QUEEN & CO.); CHIPBOARD NUMBERS (HEIDI SWAPP); EMBROIDERY FLOSS; CARDSTOCK

24/7

*Linda Harrison,
Sarasota, Florida*

Oh, the creative possibilities when you print a photo onto a transparency. Its sheer quality allows you to layer it over a design and have the pattern shine through. Linda printed three black-and-white portraits onto transparency sheets. To play upon her page theme, she layered the transparency photos over a calendar. Use this layering technique to add meaning and interest to a photo.

3.14159

2653...007932
3846...33279
5028...716939 37
51058209749445923 30781640
6286208998628034825 34211706798
21480865132823066470 938446095505
32231725359408128481117450284102701938521105559644622
22948954930381964428810975665933446128475648233
78678316527120190914564856692346034861045432664821339360726 02491412737
724587006606 55884748815209209628292540917153643678 92590360011330530 54882046652
384146951 9415116094 330572706 975990581953 0921861173 8193261179 3105118548 0744623799 8274956735 1005552724 8912279381
301194912 9833673362 4406566430 8602139494 6395224737 1907021798 6094370277 0539217176 2931767523 8467481846 7669405132 0005681271

Kevin has a goal of memorizing Pi to a hundred digits. It seems a funny goal for a fifth grader and we're not sure where he got the notion. It might have been at his school's "Pi Day" where the students celebrate the number by eating pie. He knows it to about thirty digits right now. Kevin said, "I can't see why anyone would need to know Pi past a hundred digits." Dare I admit to my eleven-year old son that I can't see why anyone needs to know Pi as long as they have a calculator with a Pi key? I'll allow him this quirk and play a sounding board for him when he wants to practice Pi.

SUPPLIES: PATTERNED PAPER (SCENIC ROUTE PAPER CO.); SELF-ADHESIVE COMPUTER FILM (CHARTPAK); DIE-CUT LETTERS (QUICKUTZ); FLUID CHALK INK; CARDSTOCK

A PIECE OF PI

Kelli Noto,
Centennial, Colorado

Get the layered look of computer-generated photo altering but in less than half the time with this technique. For a custom backdrop, Kelli printed the numbers of pi onto cardstock, leaving an oval of soft-colored numbers in the center. Next, she printed the image of her son onto self-adhesive computer film, creating a clear sticker-like photograph. She placed the photo sticker over the number background, strategically aligning her son's face over the oval of softer numbers to allow him to shine through. The result is a complex looking layered photo accomplished oh-so-simply.

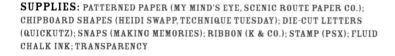

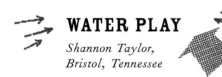

There are times in your life when you see something so unique and beautiful, that you'd can't do anything but stop and admire all of it's glory. This is what happened to me one evening. Upon arriving later than usual to the beach house, I noticed the palm tree at the corner of the porch swaying gently in the breeze, and behind it was the most glorious sunset I had ever seen. The colors were magnificent. Oranges, purples, and blues all layered upon each other, blending so delicately into the clouds. I couldn't move, I was mesmerized by its gorgeous qualities. I felt like God had created this sunset just for me to admire. I just couldn't stop staring at it. Finally, I called down to Kyle and the boys to come and look at the sky. They too saw the beauty that I did. The boys lost interest fairly soon and ran off to play, but Kyle, too, saw the uniqueness of the sky that had been bestowed upon us. We shared the moment together for awhile, and then, quickly I ran to find my camera. I didn't want to miss this opportunity to take a picture. I snapped a few photos, trying to capture my feelings in a photograph. I liked this picture the best because it highlighted my favorite palm tree, yet still showed the magnificent colors behind it. It's amazing what you see in life when you actually stop to look around and "smell the roses". If I had been scurrying about unloading the car and worrying about when I'll have the chance to go grocery shopping, I never would have seen this. What an awful thing to miss.

Photograph December 2005
Journaling May 2006

@harbor island

SUNSET @ HARBOR ISLAND

Holly Corbett,
Central, South Carolina

Let the bright colors of a photo shine through by printing it onto a transparency. Holly preserved the intense colors of a palm leaf macro shot against a vibrant sunset by printing it onto a transparency. The photo's complementary colors really pop against a monochromatic green background.

SUPPLIES: PATTERNED PAPER (MY MIND'S EYE, SCENIC ROUTE PAPER CO.); CHIPBOARD SHAPES (HEIDI SWAPP, TECHNIQUE TUESDAY); DIE-CUT LETTERS (QUICKUTZ); SNAPS (MAKING MEMORIES); RIBBON (K & CO.); STAMP (PSX); FLUID CHALK INK; TRANSPARENCY

WATER PLAY

Shannon Taylor,
Bristol, Tennessee

Easily play up photo elements with this fun transparency printing and coloring technique. Shannon printed a black-and-white photo onto a transparency sheet and then painted the back of the image with white paint to make it a bit opaque. She then highlighted photo elements by painting them with yellow, green and blue alcohol inks.

SUPPLIES: PATTERNED PAPER (BASIC GREY, JUNKITZ); PLASTIC LETTERS (HEIDI SWAPP); STRIPE COASTER (WAL-MART); ALCOHOL INKS (RANGER); TRANSPARENCY; ACRYLIC PAINT (DELTA); PIPE CLEANER; CARDSTOCK

water play

Wet & wild water play cuz hot, summer days are here to stay. Turn on the hose & let the fun splash out. Watch the kids run, scream & shout. Nothing is as fun as playing in the water on a hot, hot day that keeps getting hotter. -Oliver 2005

THERE IS LITERALLY NOTHING FOR MILES. THE HORIZON IS UNCLUTTERED BY CITY LIGHTS AND TALL BUILDINGS. THE FLAT LANDS AND SPARSE TREES LEAVE WAY FOR A MAGNIFICENT VIEW OF THE RISING FULL MOON. I STAND AND WATCH IT COME UP AND I AM INSTANTLY OVERCOME WITH A FEELING OF PEACE AND TRANQUILITY...LIKE I AM THE ONLY PERSON IN THE WHOLE WORLD... JUST ME AND THE MOON. A FEELING OF COMPLETE AND TOTAL SOLITUDE.

SUPPLIES: PATTERNED PAPER, CHIPBOARD FLOWERS, COTTON ART TAPE (IMAGINATION PROJECT); CHIPBOARD LETTERS (HEIDI SWAPP); RUB-ONS (BASIC GREY); EPOXY STICKER (PROVO CRAFT); BRADS; CARDSTOCK

SOLITUDE

Greta Hammond,
Goshen, Indiana

Get wow results with little effort with this simple printing and layering technique. Greta printed her nature photo onto white textured cardstock. She printed the same photo onto a transparency and then layered it over the cardstock-printed image. The transparency overlay intensified the image's colors, turning the sky an amazing blue with an overall dreamy effect.

a mother's love transcends space, time and even species. that bond between mama & baby orangutan was evident when we visited the zoo this spring.

As the mother grasped her baby's foot their love warmed our hearts.

baby
Love

SUPPLIES: PATTERNED PAPER (BASIC GREY); CHIPBOARD LETTERS, RUB-ONS (IMAGINATION PROJECT); CHIPBOARD HEART (HEIDI SWAPP); GOLD PEN; DYE INK; INKJET SHRINK FILM (GRAFIX); RIBBON; CARDSTOCK

BABY LOVE

Vicki Boutin,
Burlington,
Ontario, Canada

A photo printed on inkjet shrink film becomes a custom page accent. Vicki printed on inkjet shrink film the image of a mother monkey grasping her baby's foot. She then cut a slit in the film before following the manufacturer's instructions to shrink it in the oven. While the film was still warm, Vicki flattened the image with a spatula and allowed it to cool. She matted the film with beige cardstock to increase the photo's opacity and created a border with a gold leafing pen. A strung ribbon through the slit turns the small photo into an instant impact page accent.

CANVAS

 ## ROOTIN' TOOTIN'

Torrey Scott,
Thornton, Colorado

Print on burlap for a highly textural photo with true vintage appeal. Torrey cut an 8½" x 11" (22cm x 28cm) piece of burlap, and then adhered it to a sheet of cardstock of the same size with a spray adhesive. She printed her photo onto the burlap, after carefully guiding the thick material through the printer. She then sprayed the burlap photo with a sealant and removed the cardstock backing. A few pulled threads frayed the edges for a further tattered look while brads secure the photo to the background.

SUPPLIES: PATTERNED PAPER (FLAIR DESIGNS); BURLAP; BANDANA; BRADS (CREATIVE IMPRESSIONS); FELT PEN; FOAM SPACER; VELLUM ADHESIVE; ACRYLIC SEALER; CARDSTOCK; ROPE TITLE FONT (INTERNET DOWNLOAD)

SUMMER DAYS

Shannon Taylor,
Bristol, Tennessee

All eyes will be on your photo when you try this innovative printing and piecing technique. Shannon printed her sunflower image twice: once onto glossy photo paper and then onto a canvas sheet. She tore two pieces from the canvas-printed photo and then frayed the edges. She strategically placed the canvas pieces over the glossy photo. Use this cool technique to highlight photo elements and to add a touch of texture.

SUPPLIES: RIBBON, RICKRACK (SOURCE UNKNOWN); ARROW STICKERS (EK SUCCESS); LETTER STICKERS (MAKING MEMORIES); ADHESIVE; CARDSTOCK

SUPPLIES: PATTERNED PAPER (MY MIND'S EYE); GHOST LETTERS, MASK (HEIDI SWAPP); CLEAR BUTTONS, NUMBER STAMP (HERO ARTS); DIE-CUT LETTERS (QUICKUTZ); PHOTO CORNER PUNCH (EK SUCCESS); DYE INK; TRANSPARENCY; CANVAS; COLORED BUTTONS (SOURCE UNKNOWN)

FOUR

Holly Corbett,
Central, South Carolina

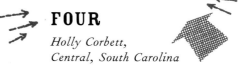

Canvas printed photos have instant art appeal, adding a soft painterly feel to any image. To achieve this work of art, Holly cut a sheet of canvas to fit onto cardstock. She then printed her photo in black-and-white onto the canvas sheet. The effect is muted and textured, adding a sense of history to a modern photo. To play up the worn look, Holly frayed the edges of the canvas and complemented it with muted patterned papers.

WEEPING WILLOWS

Sharon Laakkonen,
Superior, Wisconsin

With a sheet of canvas and a touch of a button, you can turn your photos into a French impressionistic work of art with this printing technique. Sharon began by adhering a sheet of canvas to cardstock. She then ran it through her printer to print her nature scene photo. The canvas created a highly textural and distressed looking photo. She enhanced her Monet-like masterpiece with chalks and then sealed the colorants with a fixative spray. Try this printing technique to add a painterly look to any photo.

SUPPLIES: PATTERNED PAPER (AUTUMN LEAVES, CHATTERBOX, IMAGINATION PROJECT); CHALKS (CRAF-T); RICKRACK (WAL-MART); METAL CORNERS (MICHAELS); CHIPBOARD LETTERS (LI'L DAVIS DESIGNS); DIE-CUT LETTERS (PROVO CRAFT); LEAF DESIGN (ARTIST'S OWN PATTERN); CANVAS CLOTH; WORKABLE FIXATIVES SPRAY (KRYLON); PEN; DISTRESS INK; CARDSTOCK

SUPPLIES: PATTERNED PAPER, RUB-ON TITLE (ADORN IT); ACRYLIC PAINT; BLENDER PEN, SELF-ADHESIVE COMPUTER FILM (CHARTPAK); PHOTOCOPIES (XEROX)

GIRL POWER

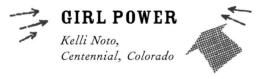

Kelli Noto,
Centennial, Colorado

Kelli added a pop-art appeal to her photo with this cool blender pen photo transfer technique. The iconic image of Kelli's young friend rockin' to her iPod called for a unique treatment, and the blender pen, also commonly referred to as a xylene pen or marker, proved to be the perfect choice. The result is a charcoal-like drawing with an Andy Warhol effect.

STEP ONE

Copy a photo onto white paper using a toner-based photo copier. Lay the image side down onto patterned paper and saturate with xylene pen.

STEP TWO

Carefully lift copy to make sure all of image has been transferred. Repeat process if necessary.

12345678

always and forever

eight years today
May 23, 2006
a day to celebrate
our love!
looking forward to
growing old
with you by my
side.
always
and
forever
we will be
together.

i love you!
Your loving wife,
Suzy
Happy Anniversary!

GOOD MEMORIES

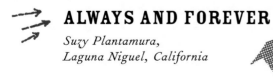

love you more every day.
xoxoxo

SUPPLIES: PATTERNED PAPER (CREATIVE IMAGINATIONS, KAREN RUSSELL); STICKERS (CREATIVE IMAGINATIONS); RUB-ONS (7 GYPSIES); CHIPBOARD LETTERS (LI'L DAVIS DESIGNS); RHINESTONE LETTERS (ME & MY BIG IDEAS); BRADS (SEI); WHITE PEN; CARDSTOCK

ALWAYS AND FOREVER

Suzy Plantamura,
Laguna Niguel, California

Suzy employed the xylene transfer technique to turn her precious photo into a vintage treasure. She wanted to add a timeless quality to the layout while reaffirming the everlasting love between her and her husband. The blender pen was quick and easy, and the result was a faded, slightly distressed looking image that works perfectly for charming photos such as this one.

LAMINATE/PACKING TAPE TRANSFER

CELEBRATE

Danielle Thompson,
Tucker, Georgia

Danielle wanted to add a touch of mystique to her photos so she used this laminate transfer technique. With just a hint of color showing through, the transparent images take on an intriguing vintage look.

celebrate

SUPPLIES: PATTERNED PAPER, SNAP BRADS, BUTTONS (AUTUMN LEAVES); LAMINATE SHEETS; FUZZY RUB-ONS (HEIDI SWAPP); RUB-ON (BASIC GREY); BLACK MARKER, PEN; CARDSTOCK

STEP ONE

Adhere a self-adhesive laminate sheet (or packing tape) over photocopy of photo. Tip: Transfer works best if photo is copied using a color copier. Inkjet images will not transfer properly.

STEP TWO

Burnish the back of the photocopy with a spoon very firmly.

STEP THREE

Soak the laminate photo in a pan of water.

STEP FOUR

Gently rub off the paper on the backside of the laminate. Be sure to not rub too hard as the transferred image can be rubbed off. Allow to dry and place on page.

You are always acting like a little scaredy cat.

You don't like dogs... not to fond of cats.

get over it

OPERATING MANUAL NOT INCLUDED

Cry if I put you in water, don't want to be barefoot.

You have to just get over it babe.

SUPPLIES: PATTERNED PAPER, BUTTONS (AUTUMN LEAVES); JELLY WORDS (MAKING MEMORIES); PACKING TAPE; CARDSTOCK

GET OVER IT

Marie Cox,
Raleigh, North Carolina

A packing tape photo transfer produces intriguing results, but a mirror-image placement of two transfers is double the fun! To create sensational visual interest, Marie adhered the two transfers in a mirrored position highlighted with a vertical row of buttons. Jounaling strips and geometric patterned paper strategically placed on each corner balance the page.

UNCONDITIONALLY

Joanna Bolick,
Fletcher, North Carolina

Joanna used a packing tape photo transfer to add a soft *trés chic* touch to this enchanting image. A subtle crackle effect resulted where the packing strips didn't completely cover the photocopy. She adhered the image to a transparency to allow the lettering on the background patterned paper to slightly shine through for an artistic effect.

SUPPLIES: PATTERNED PAPER (ANNA GRIFFIN, CREATIVE IMAGINATIONS, MELISSA FRANCES, SCRAPWORKS); TRANSPARENCY; RIBBON (A2Z ESSENTIALS); STICKERS (EK SUCCESS); PACKING TAPE; CARDSTOCK

LASTING IMPRESSION

Linda Harrison,
Sarasota, Florida

The faded look of a packing tape transfer lends a heritage touch as well as meaning to a photo. Linda used this transfer trick in conjunction with a large focal photo to drive home her page theme. The faded transfer in the lower right corner symbolizes the everlasting impression she has of her husband's smile that captures her heart each time she sees him.

SUPPLIES: LETTER RUB-ONS (ARCTIC FROG); FLOWERS (DOODLEBUG DESIGN); CHIPBOARD ACCENTS (BASIC GREY); RUB-ON ACCENTS (AUTUMN LEAVES, BASIC GREY); ACRYLIC PAINT; BUTTONS; CARDSTOCK

SUPPLIES: PATTERNED PAPER (BASIC GREY); CHIPBOARD SHAPES (FANCY PANTS DESIGNS, HEIDI SWAPP); PAINT, LEDGER PAPER, BUTTON, EMBROIDERY FLOSS (MAKING MEMORIES); CORNER ROUNDER; CHALK INK; PACKING TAPE; CARDSTOCK; ORANGE BUTTON (SOURCE UNKNOWN)

BLUE EYES

*Holly Corbett,
Central, South Carolina*

With packing tape and a little muscle, you can turn any image into a unique photo transfer. Holly achieved this cool negative-like image by applying heavy pressure to the packing tape covering the photo, but bubbles in the tape not completely burnished left shadows that created a striking underwater effect. A harmonious blend of patterned paper and accents complement her son's rosy cheeks and baby blue eyes.

GEL MEDIUM TRANSFER

HOPELESSLY IN LOVE

Shannon Taylor,
Bristol, Tennessee

A gel medium photo transfer adds a vintage touch to modern-day snapshots and creates endless possibilities for creative collage. Shannon chose this technique for the sheer quality of the photo transfer that allows the text to show through.

SUPPLIES: PATTERNED PAPER, FOAM STAMP, FLOWER BUTTONS (JUNKITZ); RUB-ONS (ME & MY BIG IDEAS); ROUND BUTTONS (DOODLEBUG DESIGN); PAINT; GEL MEDIUM (LIQUITEX); OLD BOOK PAGE; BLACK PEN; ADHESIVE; LACE (SOURCE UNKNOWN); CARDSTOCK

In his wedding vows, Andrew spoke of feeling lost and unsure of his direction in life until Cassidy came into his. In ceremonial fashion, he gazed into her eyes as he told her of his love for her and how she saved his life. You could see tears forming in both of their eyes. The same could be said for the friends and family watching from the church pews. It was quite the romantic moment.
Mr. & Mrs. Andrew Mason Burks - 2006

Anytime that is not spent on love is wasted

STEP ONE

On wax paper, place photocopy of photo face up. Paint one layer of gel medium across and just past edges. Once dry, repeat process up to four times.

STEP THREE

Once gel image transfer is dry, lightly paint another coat of gel medium onto the back of image.

STEP TWO

Peel photo from wax paper and dip into large bowl of warm water. Soak for 5-10 minutes to soften paper on back of image. Extract from water and rub back of image with fingertip until the paper is removed.

STEP FOUR

Place onto a torn page from an antique book. Apply an additional coat of gel medium to ensure it sets onto the page. Allow to dry.

SUPPLIES: PATTERNED PAPER (BASIC GREY, DAISY D'S, PROVOCRAFT); TAG (RUSTY PICKLE), RUB-ON LETTERS, COASTER HEART (IMAGINATION PROJECT); LETTER BEADS (SOURCE UNKNOWN); RIBBON (SEI); BRADS (MAKING MEMORIES); GEL MEDIUM; TRANSPARENCY; PEN

NOTEWORTHY

Deb Perry,
Newport News, Virginia

Experiment with a gel medium photo transfer to create a clearly cool image with which you can layer and unleash your creativity. Deb set her printer to "reverse print" and then printed her keyboard close-up onto matte paper. She applied gel medium over the photo, and then placed it face down onto paisley patterned paper. Deb gently rubbed the back of the photo to smooth out bubbles, and then allowed it dry for 15 minutes. She peeled back the corner of the photo to see if the image transferred, and then lightly spritzed the paper with water and rubbed it away with her finger tips.

GEL MEDIUM TRANSFER

TAKE NOTE *To create a further blurred effect, rub the edges of the transfer while adhering it to the mat.*

SUPPLIES: PATTERNED PAPER (IMAGINATION PROJECT, PRIMA); CHIPBOARD LETTERS (HEIDI SWAPP); BRADS (QUEEN & CO.); CORKBOARD FLOWERS (PRIMA); BROWN PEN; THREAD; GEL MEDIUM; DISTRESS INK; WATERCOLOR PAPER (CANSON); CARDSTOCK

COLORFUL

Sharon Laakkonen,
Superior, Wisconsin

Transform an image into a fresco-like painting with the gel medium technique. Sharon resized her floral photos in image-editing software, and then printed each onto textured paper. After transferrring each photo using the gel medium method, she carefully rubbed the edges of each so that the edges of the transferred images were not perfectly straight. This technique blended the photo into the backdrop material, making it appear like a real painting. She sealed and inked the edges of each transfer to create an aged appearance.

PRINCESSES

Kelli Noto,
Centennial, Colorado

Gel medium not only creates an ultra soft photo transfer but is also perfect for embedding shiny treasures. Kelli first made a color photo copy of her princess image. With a brush, she applied a coat of gel medium over the photo copy and then placed the image face down onto white cardstock. After the image dried, she rolled away the white copy paper, revealing the transferred image. To give the layout the perfect royal treatment, she used another coat of gel medium to embed a border of jewels, rhinestones and micro beads. Try this technique with sand, seashells and other finds for a true treasure trove.

SUPPLIES: PATTERNED PAPER (K & CO., KAREN RUSSELL); WOODEN LETTER (SOURCE UNKNOWN); DIE-CUT FLOWER AND LETTERS (QUICKUTZ); FLUID CHALK INK; WOOD STAIN (CHARTPAK); JEWELS, MIRRORS, BEADS (JEWELCRAFT); ACRYLIC PAINT; GEL MEDIUM (LIQUITEX)

GOTH

Torrey Scott,
Thornton, Colorado

A gel medium photo transfer is in itself clearly cool, but get creative with the gel application and you create grains that are beyond cool. Torrey made a laser color copy of a photo, and then smeared gel medium over the copy with vertical strokes. Once dry, she applied another coat of gel medium with horizontal strokes. She repeated the application in both directions, allowing it to dry between coats. Once thoroughly dry, Torrey soaked the copy in water, and then gently rubbed the paper from the back of the transfer. The directional variation of the gel medium application created interesting lines in the transfer.

SUPPLIES: PATTERNED PAPER (HEIDI GRACE); ACRYLIC GEL MEDIUM; RUBBER STAMPS (A STAMP IN THE HAND, JUDIKINS, STAMPABILITIES); STAMPING INK; BALL CHAIN; BRADS; SAFETY PINS; STAPLES; FOAM SPACERS; CARDSTOCK

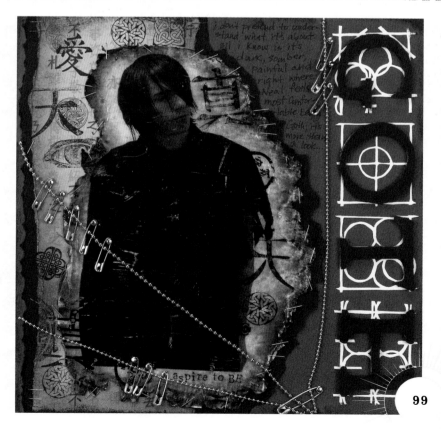

SUPPLIES: PATTERNED PAPER
(BASIC GREY); CHIPBOARD
LETTERS (HEIDI SWAPP);
CHIPBOARD PIECES (FANCY
PANTS DESIGNS); BRADS
(K & COMPANY, MAKING
MEMORIES); LABEL HOLDER,
RUB-ONS (MAKING MEMORIES);
RICKRACK (SOURCE UNKNOWN);
CARDSTOCK

DOWNTOWN CHICAGO

Greta Hammond,
Goshen, Indiana

Age a photo beyond its years with the gel medium transfer technique. Leaving just a hint of the white paper around the edges, the once modern-day photo has subdued trés chic appeal reflective of an old negative. The transparent quality of the gel medium allows the background color of the light green patterned paper to shine through creating an old world appeal perfect for a page on this topic.

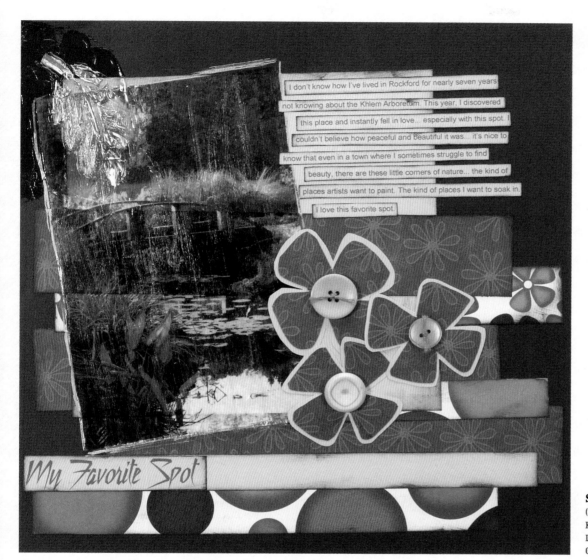

I don't know how I've lived in Rockford for nearly seven years, not knowing about the Khlem Arboretum. This year, I discovered this place and instantly fell in love... especially with this spot. I couldn't believe how peaceful and beautiful it was... it's nice to know that even in a town where I sometimes struggle to find beauty, there are these little corners of nature... the kind of places artists want to paint. The kind of places I want to soak in. I love this favorite spot.

My Favorite Spot

SUPPLIES: PATTERNED PAPER (A2Z ESSENTIALS, WE R MEMORY KEEPERS); BUTTONS (AUTUMN LEAVES); PAINT PEN; DYE INK; GEL MEDIUM; CARDSTOCK

FAVORITE SPOT

Courtney Walsh,
Winnebago, Illinois

Use gel medium to create a watercolor-like photo transfer and a dimensional design. Following the basic steps to transfer the photo, Courtney adhered the sheer image to the background with gel medium, and then applied a thick coat of gel medium to the upper corner of the image with a palette knife. She firmly impressed a rubber stamp into the gel medium for one minute. After the dimensional design dried overnight, she enhanced it with a gold paint pen.

LAZERTRAN

TAKE NOTE *The Lazertran transfer technique is great for adding an artistic touch to any image and to decoupage photo decals onto boxes, wooden plaques or other home décor.*

SUPPLIES: PATTERNED PAPER (DAISY D'S); STAMPS (SCRAPTIVITY); CHIPBOARD LETTER (BASIC GREY); RUB-ONS (SCENIC ROUTE PAPER CO.); BUTTONS, RIBBON (SOURCE UNKNOWN); PEN; GEL MEDIUM; INK; WATERSLIDE DECAL PAPER (LAZERTRAN)

SWEET DREAMS, BABY

Vicki Boutin,
Burlington,
Ontario, Canada

Take an image from ordinary to artistic with this decal transfer method. Vicki began by printing her sepia photo onto inkjet decal paper. She placed the printed image into water until the photo transferred to the decal (approximately one minute), releasing the backing sheet. Next, Vicki used a brayer to gently smooth the decal onto cardstock coated with gel medium. Once dry, she applied a coat of gel medium over the entire image and allowed it to dry overnight. The result is a trés chic finish that looks oh-so-baby soft. Vicki tore the photo's edges to lend a further aged look.

SUPPLIES: PATTERNED PAPER (AUTUMN LEAVES, KI MEMORIES); WATERSLIDE DECAL PAPER (LAZERTRAN); BUTTERFLY IMAGES (DESIGNER DIGITALS); RUB-ONS (BASIC GREY); BUTTON; EMBROIDERY FLOSS; DIE-CUT FLOWER (PAPERHOUSE PRODUCTIONS); STAMPING INK; PEN; MARKER; CARDSTOCK

THAT SOMETHING

Danielle Thompson,
Tucker, Georgia

Lend a sheer look to photos with this decal transfer technique. Danielle printed both a black-and-white and a colored photo onto water decal paper using an inkjet printer. She soaked the decal sheets in a pan of water until the image released from the backing (approximately one minute). Once the transfers were dry, she adhered the transparent decals to patterned paper using a spray adhesive. The patterned paper glows through the slightly distressed images for a cool ghost-like effect.

IRON-ON TRANSFER

I SEE A MAN WHO IS LOVED

Deb Perry,
Newport News, Virginia

A photo printed onto iron-on transfer paper becomes a sheer canvas enticing you with layering possibilities. This technique was the perfect choice for Deb who wanted to highlight her focal photo and add visual interest to her page. The sheerness of the photo transfer allows the patterned paper to shine through the image.

SUPPLIES: PATTERNED PAPER (7 GYPSIES, FIBERMARK, MELISSA FRANCES); INKJET IRON-ON TRANSFER; LETTER STICKERS, HEART COASTER, PHOTO CORNER (IMAGINATION PROJECT); RUB-ONS (K & COMPANY, KI MEMORIES); RUBBER STAMPS (RUSTY PICKLE); PEN; DIGITAL DISTRESSING (SCRAP ARTIST); FONT (DAFONT)

STEP ONE

Print photo onto inkjet printer iron-on transfer.

STEP TWO

Using a dry-heated iron, press image face down onto patterned paper. Allow to cool.

STEP THREE

Peel away paper backing to reveal the transferred image.

TAKE NOTE *Remember that images and type will transfer backwards. Follow manufacturer's instructions and print iron-on transfer in reverse if necessary.*

TAKE NOTE *For a further distressed look with this transfer technique, iron your photos onto textured cardstock.*

LLAMA TREKKING

Poor Neil. He spoils me by taking the whole family to one of my favourite places, and I repay him by dragging everyone trekking with llamas. When I told Neil I wanted to go on this excursion, he just gave me this look of disbelief. I'm sure he was hoping that I was kidding but I wasn't. I really wanted to do this. I wanted to hike through the Vermont countryside and go on a picnic that the llamas would carry for us. I know, when I say it like this, it sounds corny even to me. It sounded a lot better in the brochure.

Really it did. We actually had a good time despite the initial scepticism. The boys thought the llamas were totally cool and had an absolute blast leading their llamas along the trails and letting them stop to eat. I was so excited to be with the animals. It reminded me so much of growing up in Seattle on the farm. Neil just keep making comments under his breath about how you can take the girl out of the farm, but you can't take the farm out of the girl. He's right. You can't.

SUPPLIES: PATTERNED PAPER, RIBBON (KI MEMORIES); METAL TAG (MAKING MEMORIES); CHIP-BOARD ACCENTS (HEIDI SWAPP); DYE INK; T-SHIRT TRANSFER PAPER; CARDSTOCK; CENTURY GOTHIC, CENTURY SCHOOLBOOK FONTS (MICROSOFT)

LLAMA TREKKING

Nicole Cholet,
Beaconsfield, Quebec, Canada

The same transfer technique that allows you to wear your favorite images on a t-shirt can lend a worn retro look to photos in your scrapbook. Nicole first printed her photos onto iron-on transfer paper. Next, she used a solid flat surface, such as a wooden cutting board, to iron the transfer onto the cardstock. Once cooled, Nicole peeled off the backing paper. The transferred image looks aged by years, leaving a cool retro look.

I am free.

1 SHOT...

N.º 333

inside all of my dreams become realities & some of my realities become my dreams.

artist SHOWCASE

WITH SO MANY FUN AND FRESH TECHNIQUES to try, we knew our contributors would create some truly amazing pages. We set aside the last section to showcase the marvelous work of these talented ladies. Peruse the layouts that follow to find even more inspiration and eye-popping ways for making your photos the star of the page.

{n}

My sister, being a graduate of Clemson University, insisted on only one kind of photo for her baby announcements—this one. Baby Noah comfortably asleep in front of a Clemson football helmet, announcing to everyone his team of choice. Her husband, on the other hand, a graduate of Georgia Tech, had his concerns. Should he subject his newborn child to the abnormal tendencies of Clemson fans? But just given birth to their child, Laura won the battle, and Brian "happily" allowed such a photo. It's not difficult for a new mother to lose many battles the first few months after the baby is born. They can pretty much get away with anything, including choosing their child's preferred school of higher education eighteen years in advance!

Just how cute is **bennett** Baines? Uh.... the cutest! Not only is he a smarty, he's also VERY **good** natured! Charo & Mikey did a **super** job! And to top it all off... just look at that hair! —June 2006

the park

before turning 3.

11.2.05

on

the

your imagina

HOPE CREATE LAUGH

Talk abo

CH
CHa

true

The art of the everyday co
not lost on you. At only tw
you fill my day with discu
babies, school activities, g
eat and pony tail holders.
topic, contribute to the dis
then move on to the next
There is never awkward si
moment when you are aro
speak in complete and so
complex sentences. And yo
mastered the art of chit-ch

At the park

3 days before turning 3.

11.2.05

on the verge

your imagination knows NO bounds

HOPE CREATE LAUGH OUT LOUD REACH OUT SERVE OTHERS

Talk about wearing my heart on my sleeve...

SUPPLIES: PATTERNED PAPER (A2Z ESSENTIALS, CHATTERBOX); RUB-ONS (AMERICAN CRAFTS); RIBBON (STRANO); CARD-STOCK STICKERS (MAKING MEMORIES); STICKERS (7 GYPSIES); DIGITAL BRUSHES (DESIGNFRUIT); CARDSTOCK

ON THE VERGE

Joanna Bolick,
Fletcher, North Carolina

Add faux dimension to any photo with this image-editing trick. Joanna imported a photo into image-editing software, and then downloaded a computer brush of a floral design from the Internet. To match the brush color to the orange from her son's sweater in the photo, Joanna used the ink dropper tool. She then sized the brush to fit over the image and used the layers palette to place the brush over the photo before printing it.

SUPPLIES: PATTERNED PAPER, CHIPBOARD ACCENTS, STICKERS (SCENIC ROUTE PAPER CO.); CHIPBOARD ACCENTS (IMAGINATION PROJECT); RHINESTONE FLOWERS (SCRAPTIVITY); RHINESTONES (WESTRIM); DYE INK; PENS; FIXATIVE SPRAY; PHOTO OILS (MARSHALL'S)

YOU LEAD AND SHE WILL FOLLOW

Vicki Boutin,
Burlington, Ontario, Canada

Give a new photo heritage appeal with this bleach distressing technique. Vicki placed her photo in a bleach bath of five parts water to one part bleach for approximately two minutes. She then rinsed the photo with clean water and allowed it to dry. The bleach bath gently faded the photo, giving it a worn look. To further lend a vintage feel, Vicki applied layers of brown and yellow photo oils with cotton balls and removed the excess. Once she achieved the desired aged look, she set the photo colorants with a fixative spray.

Sam played another fantastic summer of soccer with coach Mark and the team!

an UNBELIEVABLE season!

Sam's soccer team has been playing together for 3 years now, and he wouldn't switch teams for anything. Mark is such a fantastic coach, and from him, the boys have really learned how to work together as a team. They know each other's strengths and weaknesses and they play as one (most of the time) instead of 7 individuals. That's pretty impressive for 8 year old boys!

Sam's skills have improved every year but I'm really proud of him this summer. He worked hard, even insisting on going to practices in the rain. Talk about commitment! I loved watching his games and had to laugh at how excited he got every time they won a game (which I believe, if I'm not mistaken, was all of them!) Way to go boys! Hard work really does pay off!

SUPPLIES: PATTERNED PAPER, CHIPBOARD LETTERS (SCENIC ROUTE PAPER CO.); RUB-ONS, METAL TAG (MAKING MEMORIES); RIBBON (SOURCE UNKNOWN); DYE INK; EMBOSSING POWDER; CARDSTOCK; TAHOMA FONT (MICROSOFT)

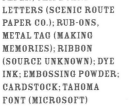

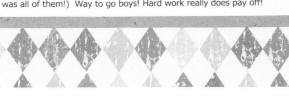

AN UNBELIEVABLE SEASON

Nicole Cholet,
Beaconsfield, Quebec, Canada

Play up the ruggedness of masculine- and sport-themed photos with this rough and tough border treatment. Nicole sanded the edges of her soccer photos until the white core was revealed to create roughed-up texture. She then inked the edges with white pigment ink for a smudged look. To mimic the grainy texture of dirt, she sprinkled the photos' edges with white embossing powder and then used a heat tool to set it.

My sister, being a graduate of Clemson University, insisted on only one kind of photo for her baby announcements—this one. Baby Noah comfortably asleep in front of a Clemson football helmet, announcing to everyone his team of choice. Her husband, on the other hand, a graduate of Georgia Tech, had his concerns. Should he subject his newborn child to the abnormal tendencies of Clemson fans? But just given birth to their child, Laura won the battle, and Brian "happily" allowed such a photo. It's not difficult for a new mother to lose many battles the first few months after the baby is born. They can pretty much get away with anything, including choosing their child's preferred school of higher education eighteen years in advance!

SUPPLIES: PATTERNED PAPERS (CHATTERBOX); FLOWERS (DOODLEBUG DESIGN, HEIDI SWAPP); NAMEPLATE (MAKING MEMORIES); FLOWER CENTER (HEIDI SWAPP); DATE STAMP; RIBBON (MAY ARTS); MINI TAGS, PHOTO CORNERS (QUICKUTZ); BRADS; INK; FLUID CHALK INK; VELLUM, CARDSTOCK, MONOGRAM "N" (SOURCE UNKNOWN)

(N)

Holly Corbett,
Central, South Carolina

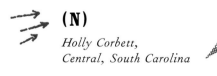

Play up a photo element that helps tell the story by highlighting it with a colorant. Though the baby is the most important part of this photo, the helmet instigates a funny story. Holly calls out the helmet by coloring it with orange chalk stamping ink applied with a cotton swab. The image is printed on a luster photo paper, adding a pearly quality to the inks.

I am a different person when I'm behind that lens...

Seeing things...capturing soon forgotten moments.

I am free.

SHOT...

N° 333

inside all of my dreams
become realities & some
of my realities become
my dreams.

SUPPLIES: PATTERNED PAPER (KI MEMORIES); RUB-ONS (7 GYPSIES); HOUSE NUMBER (HOME DEPOT); METAL MOLDING (MAKING MEMORIES); BUTTON; BRADS (DOODLEBUG DESIGN); CARDSTOCK; IMAGE EDITING SOFTWARE (ADOBE)

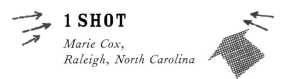

1 SHOT

Marie Cox,
Raleigh, North Carolina

Play around with image-editing software to create a custom collage with your photos. Marie changed her portrait to black-and-white in image-editing software. She selected her silhouette and then masked the background to create a blank canvas for her digital collage. Using the layers palette and several computer brushes, she layered her journaling as well as several designs over her photo. An eclectic mix of an embossed tin strip, mailbox letter, button and zigzag stitched border add even more texture and interest to the custom collage.

SUPPLIES: PATTERNED PAPER, LETTER STICKERS (BASIC GREY); PLASTIC LETTERS (HEIDI SWAPP); WHITE PEN; CARDSTOCK

GOGGLED-EYE BOY

Kelly Goree,
Shelbyville, Kentucky

Capture the true spirit of a photo by playing up its theme with design elements of wild abandon. Kelly portrayed the essence of water play in both her design choices and supply selections. She printed her focal photo to sprawl 6" x 12" (15cm x 30cm) across the page. She made good use of a large water background to float the title and waves of handwritten journaling. Torn patterned paper strips with the rough edges flailing like white caps flow across the page and carry with them small circle cropped photos that mimic beach bubbles.

SUPPLIES: PATTERNED PAPER (DAISY D'S, FONTWERKS); CHIPBOARD LETTERS AND ACCENTS (HEIDI SWAPP); RUB-ONS (AUTUMN LEAVES); COASTER FLOWER (IMAGINATION PROJECT); BRADS (MAKING MEMORIES, QUEEN & CO.); SWIRL STAMP (STAMPABILITIES); ACRYLIC PAINT; WHITE INK; CARDSTOCK

CHIT CHAT

Greta Hammond,
Goshen, Indiana

A layered look achieved with both digital and traditional scrapbooking techniques adds a powerhouse of dimension and personality to a photo. Greta started by importing her photo into image-editing software. Using the layers palette, she added a grunge mask that created the cool distressed border around the photo. She then added a digital brown mat, merged the three layers and then printed her image. Greta adhered the digital masterpiece to her page, and then further enhanced her computer-generated design with chipboard sentiments and rub-on daisies. The result is an ultra-layered look with use of only a few supplies.

Since the very day you were born you have had me in complete awe of what a naturally perfect little boy you are. In three Years, not one thing has changed.

natural wonder

SUPPLIES: CHIPBOARD LETTERS (SCENIC ROUTE PAPER CO.); DIE-CUT LETTERS (QUICKUTZ); EMBROIDERY FLOSS; BUTTERFLIES (SOURCE UNKNOWN); SAND PAPER; CRAFT KNIFE; CARDSTOCK

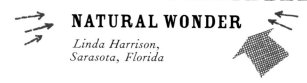

NATURAL WONDER

Linda Harrison,
Sarasota, Florida

Add wonder and whimsy to a photo with these playful touches. Linda roughed up the edges of her enlarged photo with sandpaper to lend a rugged, boyish feel. With a pen, she sketched a butterfly path from the background paper onto the photo, and then hand stitched over the pattern with a needle and embroidery floss. Butterflies mounted at the end of each path flutter on the photo. Die-cut letters spell out vertical journaling that carries the eye from the photo through the page.

SUPPLIES: RIBBON, PAPER FLOWERS (PRIMA); PHOTO CORNERS, LETTER RUB-ONS (IMAGINATION PROJECT); ACRYLIC LETTERS, FLOWER GEMS (HEIDI SWAPP); BEADS (MICHAELS); WHITE PEN; LIQUID ADHESIVE; STAMPING INK; THREAD; CORNER ROUNDER; CARDSTOCK

SO ELEGANT

Sharon Laakkonen,
Superior, Wisconsin

Add a touch of sparkle and elegance to your photos with hand stitching and beadwork. Sharon stitched and adhered beads directly to the photo to enhance the detail of the dresses. Flower beads and crystal gems draw attention to the girls' up-dos. A frame of blue stitches and beads adhered to photo corners further dress up the photo. A beaded title and a stitched border tie Sharon's photo-handiwork to the page.

Grand Canyon

ADVENTURE

March, 2006

Four teenage boys on the edge of adventure. Even though they prepared for this trip, they still didn't know just how difficult the ten-mile trek would be. The pack mules carried most of the gear and food, but each of the boys still hauled a thirty-pound backpack along switchback trails and through narrow canyons. They reached the campground after seven hours of hiking. Their shoulders rubbed raw, every muscle ached, and their feet sported blisters the size of quarters. They staggered into camp exhausted but exhilarated, ready to enjoy the next week deep inside the Grand Canyon and away from all worries except the eventual hike back up!

SUPPLIES: PATTERNED PAPER (ADORN IT); DIE-CUT LETTERS, DIE-CUT NUMBERS (QUICKUTZ); RUB-ON LETTERS (CREATIVE IMAGINATIONS); ACRYLIC PAINT; FLUID CHALK INK; CARDSTOCK

GRAND CANYON ADVENTURE

*Kelli Noto,
Centennial, Colorado*

Use this clever painting technique to imitate the look of an artistic computer-generated border, but in half the time. Using a piece of cardstock dipped into black paint, Kelli created this grungy yet artsy border directly onto her photo in seconds flat. Then with the brush of her finger, Kelli brushed paint onto the edges of the photo for further definition.

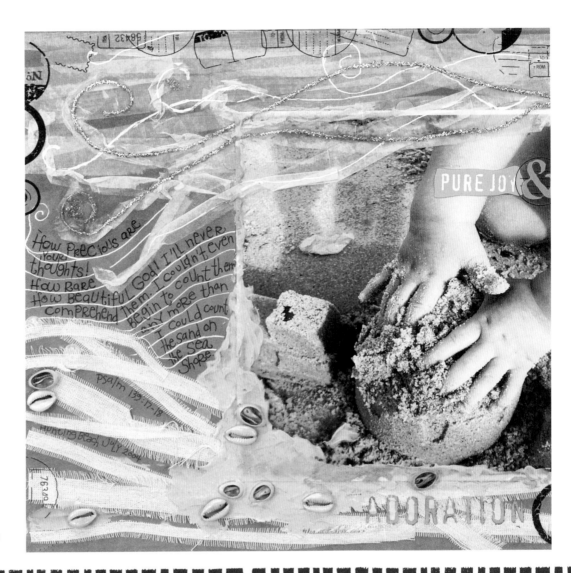

SUPPLIES: GEL MEDIUM; TISSUE PAPER; FABRIC FIBERS (FIBERMARK); SAND (MAGICSCRAPS); SHELLS (SOURCE UNKNOWN); PAINT; RUB-ONS (K & COMPANY); PEN; CARDSTOCK

ADORATION

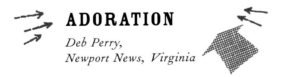

Deb Perry,
Newport News, Virginia

Purposefully planned and placed embellishments continued from the background onto the photo can enhance a page theme with design continuity. Deb simulated sand on the background paper with sewed frayed fabric strips that visually move into a patch of gel medium sprinkled with sand on the photo. Torn tissue paper strips adhered with decoupage medium and then enhanced with glitter fibers emulate reflective water flowing across the top of the page, spilling onto the photo.

SUPPLIES: PATTERNED PAPER (AUTUMN LEAVES, SANDYLION); CHIPBOARD LETTERS (LI'L DAVIS DESIGNS); LARGE MONO-GRAM LETTER (BAZZILL); RHINESTONES (K & COMPANY); WHITE PEN; MARKERS; GEL MEDIUM

IT'S CALLED ATTITUDE...

Suzy Plantamura,
Laguna Niguel, California

Get creative with a gel medium transfer to add customized texture and design to your photos. Suzy brushed on three applications of gel medium to this sassy photo, allowing it to dry between coats. With her finger, she thickly spread on a wavy fourth coat, and let it dry for two days. Suzy then immersed the photo into warm water and gently rubbed off the paper backing. She placed flower cutouts on textured cardstock, and then adhered the transferred image on top. The transparent image allows the punchy flower cutouts to peek through.

SUPPLIES: PATTERNED PAPER (FRANCES MEYER); CHIPBOARD LETTERS AND ACCENTS (EK SUCCESS); GLAZE PEN (SAKURA); FELT PEN; FOAM SPACERS; IMAGE EDITING SOFTWARE (ADOBE); CARDSTOCK

ADORE

Torrey Scott, Thornton, Colorado
Photo and journaling: Jodi Amidei, Lafayette, Colorado

Put the spotlight on a photo subject with this creative journaling and matting technique. Torrey extended the background of her photo in image-editing software to accommodate the journaling. With a cutting knife and patterned paper, she created a scrolly mat to mimic hair curls. Handwritten journaling directly on the photo follows the curves of the mat while highlighting the subject's cheeky grin.

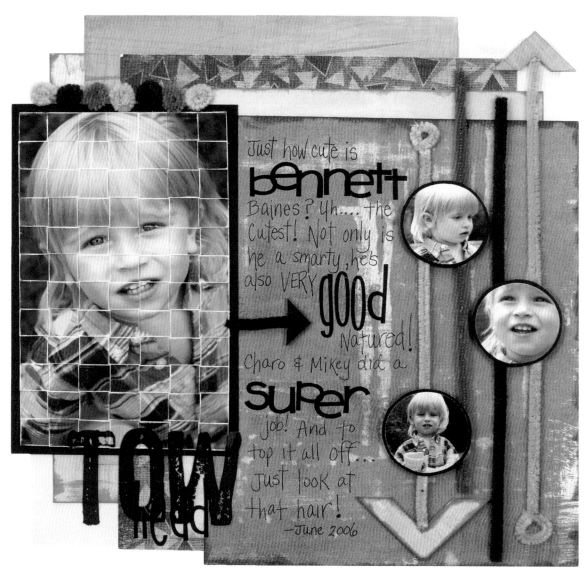

Just how cute is **bennett** Baines? Uh.....the Cutest! Not only is he a smarty, he's also VERY **good** Natured! Charo & Mikey did a **SUPER** job! And to top it all off... Just look at that hair!

—June 2006

TOW head

SUPPLIES: PATTERNED PAPER (BASIC GREY, JUNKITZ); LETTER STICKERS AND RUB-ONS, CHIPBOARD ACCENTS (JUNKITZ); PIPE CLEANERS; STAMPING INK; FOAM SQUARES

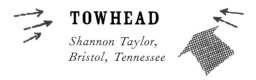

TOWHEAD

Shannon Taylor,
Bristol, Tennessee

To showcase a photograph with true pizzazz, try this photo weaving technique. Shannon printed the same photo twice. With scissors, she cut one photo into horizontal strips and the other into vertical strips all of the same width. Then she lightly sanded the edges of each strip. Shannon wove the two photos together, placing a dot of adhesive at each overlap to ensure a tight weave.

SUPPLIES: PATTERNED PAPER (BASIC GREY); DIGITAL BRUSHES (SCRAP ARTIST); IMAGE EDITING SOFTWARE (ADOBE); FABRIC FOR PHOTO CORNER (JO-ANN STORES); RUB-ONS, EPOXY STICKERS (AUTUMN LEAVES); EMBROIDERY FLOSS; MARKER; PEN; CARDSTOCK

KATIE

Danielle Thompson,
Tucker, Georgia

Mix digital techniques with handmade touches to create an artsy photo collage with lots of eye candy. In image-editing software, Danielle used digital brushes to layer a swirly border and a lacey frame over her photos. After printing the photos, she cut out the smallest one from the collage and mounted it with dimensional adhesive to make it pop from the page. Floral rub-ons and freehand scrolls add further fancy to the photos. A crumpled photo corner cut from patterned paper is stitched over one of the photos, adding a textural touch.

cute
fun
perfect

the
dress

SUPPLIES: PATTERNED
PAPER (CHATTERBOX); LETTER
STICKERS (AMERICAN CRAFTS,
SEI); EMBROIDERY FLOSS (DMC);
BUTTONS (AUTUMN LEAVES);
PEN; CARDSTOCK

THE DRESS

Courtney Walsh,
Winnebago, Illinois

Call out a favorite photo with a homespun stitched frame. Courtney matted her focal photo onto
a mix of patterned paper squares. Then she used a ruler and a pencil to measure and mark around
the photo where she wanted to stitch the frame. With contrasting embroidery floss and a needle,
Courtney stitched two rows of straight stitches to frame the photo. Buttons and additional
stitching add a sweet touch and lots of texture to the layout.

The following companies manufacture products featured in this book. Please check your local retailers to find these materials, or go to a company's Web site for the latest product. In addition, we have made every attempt to properly credit the items mentioned in this book. We apologize to any company that we have listed incorrectly, and we would appreciate hearing from you.

SOURCE GUIDE

3L Corporation
(800) 828-3130
www.scrapbook-adhesives.com

3M
(800) 364-3577
www.3m.com

7 Gypsies
(877) 749-7797
www.sevengypsies.com

A2Z Essentials
(419) 663-2869
www.a2zessentials.com

AccuCut®
(800) 288-1670
www.accucut.com

Adobe Systems Incorporated
(866) 766-2256
www.adobe.com

Adorn It / Carolee's Creations
(435) 563-1100
www.adornit.com

Advantus Corp.
(904) 482-0091
www.advantus.com

All My Memories
(888) 553-1998
www.allmymemories.com

American Crafts
(801) 226-0747
www.americancrafts.com

Anima Designs
(412) 726-8401
www.animadesigns.com

Anna Griffin, Inc.
(888) 817-8170
www.annagriffin.com

Arctic Frog
(479) 636-FROG
www.arcticfrog.com

Around The Block
(801) 593-1946
www.aroundtheblockproducts.com

Artgirlz
(401) 323-2997
www.artgirlz.com

Autumn Leaves
(800) 588-6707
www.autumnleaves.com

Avery Dennison Corporation
(800) 462-8379
www.avery.com

Basic Grey™
(801) 451-6006
www.basicgrey.com

Bazzill Basics Paper
(480) 558-8557
www.bazzillbasics.com

Beacon Adhesives
(914) 699-3405
www.beaconcreates.com

Beadery®, The
(401) 539-2432
www.thebeadery.com

Berwick Offray™, LLC
(800) 344-5533
www.offray.com

Blumenthal Lansing Company
(201) 935-6220
www.buttonsplus.com

Bo-Bunny Press
(801) 771-4010
www.bobunny.com

Brother® International Corporation
www.brother.com

Canon U.S.A., Inc.
(800) 652-2666
www.canon.com

Canson®, Inc.
(800) 628-9283
www.canson-us.com

Canvas Concepts™
(800) 869-7220
www.canvasconcepts.com

CARL Mfg. USA, Inc.
(800) 257-4771
www.Carl-Products.com

Carolee's Creations® - see Adorn It

ChartPak
(800) 628-1910
www.chartpak.com

Chatterbox, Inc.
(208) 939-9133
www.chatterboxinc.com

Cherry Arte
(212) 465-3495
www.cherryarte.com

Clearsnap, Inc.
(888) 448-4862
www.clearsnap.com

Cloud 9 Design
(866) 348-5661
www.cloud9design.biz

Club Scrap™, Inc.
(888) 634-9100
www.clubscrap.com

Colorbök™, Inc.
(800) 366-4660
www.colorbok.com

Cosmo Cricket
(800) 852-8810
www.cosmocricket.com

Craf-T Products
(507) 235-3996
www.craf-tproducts.com

Crate Paper
(702) 966-0409
www.cratepaper.com

Crayola®
(800) 272-9652
www.crayola.com

Creative Imaginations
(800) 942-6487
www.cigift.com

Dafont
www.dafont.com

Daisy D's Paper Company
(888) 601-8955
www.daisydspaper.com

Darice, Inc.
(800) 321-1494
www.darice.com

Dèjá Views
(800) 243-8419
www.dejaviews.com

Delta Technical Coatings, Inc.
(800) 423-4135
www.deltacrafts.com

Deluxe Designs
(480) 497-9005
www.deluxecuts.com

Designer Digitals
www.designerdigitals.com

Design Originals
(800) 877-0067
www.d-originals.com

Designfruit
(417) 838-6832
www.designfruit.com

Die Cuts With A View
(801) 224-6766
www.diecutswithaview.com

DMC Corp.
(973) 589-0606
www.dmc.com

Doodlebug Design™ Inc.
(801) 966-9952
www.doodlebug.ws

Dymo
(800) 426-7827
www.dymo.com

Eastman Kodak Company
(770) 522-2542
www.kodak.com

EK Success™, Ltd.
(800) 524-1349
www.eksuccess.com

Ellison®
(800) 253-2238
www.ellison.com

Elmer's Products, Inc.
(800) 848-9400
www.elmers.com

Epson America, Inc.
(562) 981-3840
www.epson.com

Fancy Pants Designs, LLC
(801) 779-3212
www.fancypantsdesigns.com

FiberMark
(802) 257-0365
http://scrapbook.fibermark.com

Fiskars®, Inc.
(866) 348-5661
www.fiskars.com

Flair® Designs
(888) 546-9990
www.flairdesignsinc.com

FontWerks
(604) 942-3105
www.fontwerks.com

Foss Manufacturing
(800) 746-4020
www.fossmfg.com

Frances Meyer, Inc.®
(413) 584-5446
www.francesmeyer.com

Fuji Photo Film U.S.A., Inc.
(800) 755-3854
www.fujifilm.com

gel•a•tins
(800) 393-2151
www.gelatinstamps.com

Go West Studios
(214) 227-0007
www.goweststudios.com

Grafix®
(800) 447-2349
www.grafix.com

Hambly Studios
(800) 451-3999
www.hamblystudios.com

Hampton Art Stamps, Inc.
(800) 229-1019
www.hamptonart.com

Happy Hammer, The
(720) 870-5248
www.thehappyhammer.com

Heidi Grace Designs, Inc.
(608) 294-4509
www.heidigrace.com

Heidi Swapp/Advantus Corporation
(904) 482-0092
www.heidiswapp.com

Heritage Scrapbooks
(888) 622-6556
www.heritagescrapbooks.com

Hero Arts® Rubber Stamps, Inc.
(800) 822-4376
www.heroarts.com

Home Depot
www.homedepot.com

Hot Off The Press, Inc.
(800) 227-9595
www.b2b.hotp.com

Imagination Project, Inc.
(513) 860-2711
www.imaginationproject.com

Impress Rubber Stamps
(206) 901-9101
www.impressrubberstamps.com

Inkadinkado® Rubber Stamps
(800) 888-4652
www.inkadinkado.com

JewelCraft, LLC
(201) 223-0804
www.jewelcraft.biz

Jo-Ann Stores
(888) 739-4120
www.joann.com

JudiKins
(310) 515-1115
www.judikins.com

Junkitz™
(732) 792-1108
www.junkitz.com

K & Company
(888) 244-2083
www.kandcompany.com

Kaleidoscope Collections, LLC
(970) 231-4076
www.kaleidoscopecollections.com

Karen Russell
www.karenrussell.typepad.com

Keepsake Designs
(207) 324-0883
www.keepsakedesigns.biz

KI Memories
(972) 243-5595
www.kimemories.com

Kolo® LLC
(888) 636-5656
www.kolo.com

Krylon®
(216) 566-200
www.krylon.com

Lä Dé Dä
(225) 755-8899
www.ladeda.com

Lasting Impressions for Paper, Inc.
(801) 298-1979
www.lastingimpressions.com

Lazar Studiowerx, Inc.
(866) 478-9379
www.lazarstudiowerx.com

Lazartran L.L.C.
(800) 245-7547
www.lazartran.com

Li'l Davis Designs
(949) 838-0344
www.lildavisdesigns.com

Lindy's Stamp Gang
(360) 785-4588
www.lindystampgang.com

Liquitex® Artist Materials
(888) 4-ACRYLIC
www.liquitex.com

Little Black Dress Designs
(360) 897-8844
www.littleblackdressdesigns.com

Loew-Cornell, Inc.
(201) 836-7070
www.loew-cornell.com

Magenta Rubber Stamps
(450) 922-5253
www.magentastyle.com

Magic Mesh
(651) 345-6374
www.magicmesh.com

Magic Scraps™
(972) 238-1838
www.magicscraps.com

MaisyMo™ Designs
(973) 907-7262
www.maisymo.com

Making Memories
(800) 286-5263
www.makingmemories.com

Mara-Mi, Inc.
(800) 627-2648
www.mara-mi.com

Ma Vinci's Reliquary -
no source available

May Arts
(800) 442-3950
www.mayarts.com

Maya Road, LLC
(214) 488-3279
www.mayaroad.com

me & my BiG ideas®
(949) 883-2065
www.meandmybigideas.com

Memories Complete™, LLC
(866) 966-6365
www.memoriescomplete.com

Melissa Frances/Heart & Home, Inc.
(905) 686-9031
www.melissafrances.com

Michaels® Arts & Crafts
(800) 642-4235
www.michaels.com

Midori
(800) 659-3049
www.midoriribbon.com

MOD-my own design
(303) 641-8680
www.mod-myowndesign.com

Mustard Moon™
(763) 493-5157
www.mustardmoon.com

My Mind's Eye™, Inc.
(800) 665-5116
www.frame-ups.com

My Sentiments Exactly
(719) 260-6001
www.sentiments.com

NRN Designs
(800) 421-6958
www.nrndesigns.com

Nunn Design
(360) 379-3557
www.nunndesign.com

Offray - see Berwick Offray, LLC

Pageframe Designs
(877) 553-7263
www.scrapbookframe.com

Paper Heart Studio
(904) 230-8108
www.paperheartstudio.com

Paper House Productions®
(800) 255-7316
www.paperhouseproductions.com

Paper Patch®, The
(800) 397-2737
www.paperpatch.com

Paper Salon
(952) 445-6878
www.papersalon.com

Paper Studio
(480) 557-5700
www.paperstudio.com

Penny Black, Inc.
www.pennyblackinc.com

Plaid Enterprises, Inc.
(800) 842-4197
www.plaidonline.com

Pressed Petals
(800) 748-4656
www.pressedpetals.com

Prickley Pear Rubber Stamps
www.prickleypear.com

Prima Marketing, Inc.
(909) 627-5532
www.mulberrypaperflowers.com

Prism™ Papers
(866) 902-1002
www.prismpapers.com

Provo Craft®
(888) 577-3545
www.provocraft.com

PSX Design™
(800) 782-6748
www.psxdesign.com

Queen & Co.
(858) 485-5132
www.queenandcompany.com

Quest Beads & Cast, Inc.
(212) 354-0979
www.questbeads.com

QuicKutz, Inc.
(801) 765-1144
www.quickutz.com

Ranger Industries, Inc.
(800) 244-2211
www.rangerink.com

Ribbon Smyth
(215) 249-9096
www.ribbonsmyth.com

Royal® & Langnickel/Royal Brush Mfg.
(219) 660-4170
www.royalbrush.com

Rusty Pickle
(801) 746-1045
www.rustypickle.com

Sakura Hobby Craft
(310) 212-7878
www.sakuracraft.com

Sandylion Sticker Designs
(800) 387-4215
www.sandylion.com

Sassafras Lass
(801) 269-1331
www.sassafraslass.com

Savvy Stamps
(866) 447-2889
www.savvystamps.com

Scenic Route Paper Co.
(801) 785-0761
www.scenicroutepaper.com

Scrap Artist
www.scrapartist.com

ScrapGoods™
(866) 554-6895
www.scrapgoods.com

Scrapperware - no source available

Scraptivity™ Scrapbooking, Inc.
(800) 393-2151
www.scraptivity.com

Scrapworks, LLC
(801) 363-1010
www.scrapworks.com

Scrappy Doodles
(877) 835-5960
www.scrappydoodles.com

SEI, Inc.
(800) 333-3279
www.shopsei.com

Shoebox Trims
(303) 257-7578
www.shoeboxtrims.com

Sonnets
www.store.scrapbook.com/sonnets

Stamp in the Hand Co., A
(310) 515-4818
www.astampinthehand.com

Stampa Rosa - no source available

Stampabilities®
(800) 888-0321
www.stampabilities.com

Stampin' Up!®
(800) 782-6787
www.stampinup.com

Sticker Studio™
(208) 322-2465
www.stickerstudio.com

Strano Designs
(508) 454-4615
www.stranodesigns.com

Strathmore Papers
(also see Mohawk Paper Mills)
(800) 628-8816
www.strathmore.com

Target
www.target.com

Technique Tuesday, LLC
(503) 644-4073
www.techniquetuesday.com

Teters Floral Product
(800) 999-5996
www.teters.com

Therm O Web, Inc.
(800) 323-0799
www.thermoweb.com

Treehouse Designs
(888) 468-4832
www.treehouse-designs.com

Tsukineko®, Inc.
(800) 769-6633
www.tsukineko.com

Two Peas in a Bucket
(888) 896-7327
www.twopeasinabucket.com

Uniball
www.uniball.com

Urban Lily
www.urbanlily.com

USArtQuest, Inc.
(517) 522-6225
www.usartquest.com

Vintage Workshop® LLC, The
(913) 341-5559
www.thevintageworkshop.com

VWR™ International
(800) 932-5000
www.vwr.com

Wagner
(800) 328-8251
www.wagnerspraytech.com

Wal-Mart Stores, Inc.
(800) WALMART
www.walmart.com

We R Memory Keepers, Inc.
(801) 539-5000
www.weronthenet.com

Westrim® Crafts
(800) 727-2727
www.westrimcrafts.com

Xerox
www.xerox.com

INDEX

LEARN MORE WITH THESE FINE TITLES FROM MEMORY MAKERS AND NORTH LIGHT BOOKS!

Learn from scrapbook artist Trudy Sigurdson on how to begin a journey into capturing emotion on scrapbook pages through the use of poems, quotes and sayings.

ISBN-13: 978-1-892127-84-6
ISBN-10: 1-892127-84-9

paperback, 112 pgs., #Z0023, $19.99

Discover how to create extraordinary photos that will make any scrapbook or display project a vivid record of special events and everyday life.

ISBN-13: 978-1-58180-909-1
ISBN-10: 1-58180-909-3

paperback, 128 pgs., #Z0526, $22.99

Open the pages of this colossal gallery and discovery over 500 amazing page layouts plus 75 printage sketches on bonus CD-Rom.

ISBN-13: 978-1-892127-91-4
ISBN-10: 1-892127-91-1

paperback, 224 pgs., #Z0349, $24.99